The Quare Fellow

A COMEDY-DRAMA

Brendan Behan

METHUEN & CO LTD

11 NEW FETTER LANE · LONDON EC4

First published in 1956 by arrangement with
Progress House (Publications) Ltd.
270 North Circular Road, Dublin
First paperback edition 1960
Reprinted four times
Reprinted 1970
SBN 416 62920 2
1·6

Printed in Great Britain by
John Dickens and Co Ltd Northampton

*This version of "The Quare Fellow" was first presented
by Theatre Workshop at the Theatre Royal, Stratford,
London, E.15, on 24th May 1956, with the following
cast:*

PRISONERS

Dunlavin	Maxwell Shaw
Neighbour	Gerard Dynevor
Prisoner A. (*Hard Case*)	Glynn Edwards
Prisoner B. (*The Man of Thirty*)	Brian Murphy
Lifer	Bill Grover
The Other Fellow	Ron Brooker
Mickser	Eric Ogle
English Voice	John Rutley
Scholara ⎱ (*Young Prisoners*) ⎰	Timothy Harley
Shaybo ⎰ ⎱	George Eugeniou
Prisoner C. (*The Boy from the Island*)	Henry Livings
Prisoner D. (*The Embezzler*)	Barry Clayton
Prisoner E. (*The Bookie*)	Brian Murphy

WARDERS

Chief Warder	Maxwell Shaw
Regan	Dudley Foster
Crimmin	Brian Nunn
Donelly (*Warder 1*)	Clive Goodwin
The New One (*Warder 2*)	Fred Cooper
The Prison Governor	Robert Henderson
Holy Healey	Barry Clayton
The Hangman	Gerry Raffles
Jenkinson	Brian Murphy

The play directed by Joan Littlewood

ACT I

A prisoner sings: he is in one of the punishment cells.

A hungry feeling came o'er me stealing
And the mice were squealing in my prison cell,
And that old triangle
Went jingle jangle,
Along the banks of the Royal Canal.

The curtain rises.

*The scene is the bottom floor or landing of a wing in a
city prison, "B.1". The cell doors are of metal with a
card giving the name, age and religion of the occupant.
Two of the cells have no cards. The left of the stage
leads to the circle, the administrative heart of the
prison, and on the right, in the wall and at right
angles to the audience, is a window, from which
a view may be had of the laundry yard of the women's
prison. On the wall and facing the audience is printed
in large block shaded Victorian lettering the word
"SILENCE".*

PRISONER.

To begin the morning
The warder bawling
Get out of bed and clean up your cell,
And that old triangle
Went jingle jangle,
Along the banks of the Royal Canal.

1

A triangle is beaten, loudly and raucously. A WARDER *comes briskly and, swinging a bunch of keys, goes to the vacant cells, looks in the spyholes, takes two white cards from his pocket, and puts one on each door. Then he goes to the other doors, looks in the spyholes and unlocks them.*

Meanwhile the singer in the base punishment cells is on his third verse:

> The screw was peeping
> And the lag was weeping . . .

But this only gets as far as the second line, for the warder leans over the stairs and shouts down . . .

WARDER. The screw is listening as well as peeping, and you'll be bloody well weeping if you don't give over your moaning. We might go down there and give you something to moan about. [*The singing stops and he turns and shouts up and down the landing.*] B. Wings: two, three and one. Stand to your doors. Come on, clean up your cells there. [*He goes off* R.]

PRISONERS A. *and* B. *come out of their cells, collect buckets and brushes, and start the morning's chores.* A. *is a man of 40, he has done two "laggings", a sentence of five years or more, and some preventive detention.* B. *is a gentle-looking man and easy-going.*

PRISONER A. Nice day for the races.

PRISONER B. Don't think I can make it today. Too much to do in the office. Did you hear the commotion last night round in D. Wing? A reprieve must have come through.

PRISONER A. Aye, but there's two for a haircut and shave, I wonder which one's been chucked?

PRISONER B. Dunlavin might know; give him a call there.

PRISONER A. Dunlavin!

VOICE [*from cell*].

> There are hands that will welcome you in
> There are lips that I am burning to kiss
> There are two eyes that shine . . .

PRISONER A. Hey, Dunlavin, are you going to scrub that place of yours away?

VOICE.

> Far away where the blue shadows fall
> I will come to contentment and rest,
> And the toils of the day
> Will be all charmed away . . .

PRISONER A. Hey, Dunlavin.

DUNLAVIN *appears in the door of the cell polishing a large enamel chamber pot with a cloth. An old man, he has spent most of his life in jail. Unlike most old lags he has not become absolutely dulled from imprisonment.*

DUNLAVIN. . . . In my little grey home in the West.

PRISONER A. What do you think that is you're polishing—the Railway Cup?

DUNLAVIN. I'm shining this up for a special visitor. Healey of the Department of Justice is coming up today to inspect the cells.

PRISONER A. Will he be round again so soon?

DUNLAVIN. He's always round the day before an execution. I think he must be in the hanging and flogging section.

PRISONER B. Dunlavin, there you are, at the corner of the wing, with the joints in the hot-water pipes bringing you news from every art and part, any time you put your ear to it.

DUNLAVIN. Well? Well?

PRISONER B. Well, what was the commotion last night round in D. Wing? Did the quare fellow get a reprieve?

DUNLAVIN. Just a minute till I put back me little bit of china, and I'll return and tell all. Now which quare fellow do you mean? The fellow beat his wife to death with the silver-topped cane, that was a presentation to him from the Combined Staffs, Excess and Refunds branch of the late Great Southern Railways, was reprieved, though why him any more than the other fellow is more nor I can tell.

PRISONER A. Well, I suppose they looked at it, he only killed her and left it at that. He didn't cut the corpse up afterwards with a butcher's knife.

DUNLAVIN. Yes, and then of course the other fellow used a meat-chopper. Real bog-man act. Nearly as bad as a shotgun, or getting the weed-killer mixed up in the stir-about. But a man with a silver-topped cane, that's a man that's a cut above meat-choppers whichever way you look at it.

PRISONER A. Well, I suppose we can expect Silver-top round soon to start his life.

PRISONER B. Aye, we've a couple of vacancies.

PRISONER A. There's a new card up here already.

DUNLAVIN. I declare to God you're right. [*Goes to read one of the cards.*] It's not him at all, it's another fellow, doing two year, for . . . oh, the dirty beast, look what the dirty man-beast is in for. 'Clare to God, putting the likes of that beside me. They must think this is the bloody sloblands.

PRISONER B. There's another fellow here.

DUNLAVIN. I hope it's not another of that persuasion. [*Reads the card.*] Ah, no, it's only the murderer, thanks be to God.

The others have a read of the card and skip back to their own cells.

DUNLAVIN. You wouldn't mind old Silver-top. Killing your wife is a natural class of a thing could happen to the best of us. But this other dirty animal on me left . . .

PRISONER B. Ah well, now he's here he'll just have to do his birdlime like anyone else.

DUNLAVIN. That doesn't say that he should do it in the next flowery dell to me. Robbers, thieves and murderers I can abide, but when it comes to that class of carry-on— Good night, Joe Doyle.

PRISONER A. [*indicates 22*]. This fellow was dead lucky.

PRISONER B. Live lucky.

PRISONER A. Two fellows waiting to be topped and he's the one that gets away. As a general rule they don't like reprieving one and topping the other.

DUNLAVIN. So as to be on the safe side, and not to be making fish of one and flesh of the other, they usually top both. Then, of course, the Minister might have said, enough is as good as a feast.

They rest on their brooms.

PRISONER B. It must be a great thing to be told at the last minute that you're not going to be topped after all. To be lying there sweating and watching. The two screws for the death watch coming on at twelve o'clock and the two going off shaking hands with you, and you go to bed, and stare up at the ceiling.

DUNLAVIN. And the two screws nod to each other across the fire to make a sup of tea, but to do it easy in case they wake you, and you turn round in the bed towards the fire and you say "I'll take a sup as you're at it" and one of the screws says "Ah, so you're awake, Mick. We were just wetting it; isn't it a good job you spoke up in time."

PRISONER A. And after that, the tea is drunk and they offer you cigarettes, though the mouth is burned off you from smoking and anyway you've more than they have, you've got that many you'll be leaving them after you, and you lie down and get up, and get up and lie down, and the two screws not letting on to be minding you and not taking their eyes off you for one half-minute, and you walk up and down a little bit more . . .

PRISONER B. And they ask you would you like another game of draughts or would you sooner write a letter, and getting on to morning you hear a bell out in the city, and you ask them the time, but they won't tell you.

DUNLAVIN. But they put a good face on it, and one says "There's that old watch stopped again" and he says to the other screw "Have you your watch, Jack?" and the other fellow makes a great joke of it, "I'll have to take a run up as far as the North City Pawn shop and ask them to let me have a look at it." And then the door is unlocked and everyone sweats blood, and they come in and ask your man to stand up a minute, that's if he's able, while they read him something: "I am instructed to inform you that the Minister has, he hasn't, he has, he hasn't recommended to the President, that . . ."

PRISONER A. And the quare fellow says "Did you say 'has recommended or has not recommended. . . ?' I didn't quite catch that."

DUNLAVIN. My bloody oath but he catches it. Although I remember once in a case like now when there were two fellows to be topped over two different jobs, didn't the bloody fellow from the Prison Board, as it was then, in old Max Greeb's time, didn't he tell the wrong man he was reprieved? Your man was delighted for a few hours and then they had to go back and tell him "Sorry, my mistake, but you're to be topped after all"?

PRISONER B. And the fellow that was reprieved, I bet he was glad.

DUNLAVIN. Of course he was glad, anyone that says that a condemned man would be better off hung than doing life, let them leave it to his own discretion. Do you know who feels it worse going out to be topped?

PRISONER A. Corkmen and Northerners . . . they've such bloody hard necks.

DUNLAVIN. I have to do me funny half-hour for Holy Healey. I'm talking serious now.

PRISONER A. All right, come on, let's have it—

DUNLAVIN. The man that feels it worst, going into that little house with the red door and the silver painted gates at the bottom of D. Wing, is a man that has been in the nick before, when some other merchant was topped; or he's heard screws or old lags in the bag shop or at exercise talking about it. A new chap that's never done anything but murder, and that only once, is usually a respectable man, such as this Silver-top here. He knows nothing about it, except the few lines that he'd see in the papers. "Condemned man entered the hang-house at seven fifty-nine. At eight three the doctor pronounced life extinct."

PRISONER B. That's a lot of mullarkey. In the first place the doctor has his back turned after the trap goes down, and doesn't turn and face it until a screw has caught the rope and stopped it wriggling. Then they go out and lock up the shop and have their breakfast and don't come back for an hour. Then they cut your man down and the doctor slits the back of his neck to see if the bones are broken. Who's to know what happens in the hour your man is swinging there, maybe wriggling to himself in the pit.

PRISONER A. You're right there. When I was in the nick in England, there was a screw doing time, he'd been smuggling out medical reports on hangings and selling them to the Sunday papers, and he told me that one bloke had lived seventeen minutes at the end of a rope.

DUNLAVIN. I don't believe that! Seventeen minutes is a bloody long time to be hanging on the end of a rope.

PRISONER A. It was their own medical report.

PRISONER B. I'll lay odds to a make that Silver-top isn't half charmed with himself he's not going with the meat-chopper in the morning.

DUNLAVIN. You could sing that if you had an air to it.

PRISONER A. They'll have him down to reception, changed into Fry's and over here any time now.

DUNLAVIN. Him and this other jewel here. Bad an' all as Silver-top was to beat his wife's brains out, I'd as lief have him near to me as this article. Dirty beast! I won't have an hour's luck for the rest of me six months, and me hoping to touch Uncle Healey today for a letter to the Room-Keepers for when I'd go out.

PRISONER B. Eh, Dunlavin, is the Department trying to reform, reconstruct and rehabilitate you in your old age?

DUNLAVIN. Ah no, it's nothing to do with the Department. Outside his job in the Department, Uncle Healey's in some holy crowd, that does good be stealth. They never let the right hand know what the left hand doeth, as the man said. Of course they never put either hand in their pocket, so you'd never get money off them, but they can give letters to the Prisoners' Aid and the Room-Keepers. Mind you. Healey's not here today as a holy man. He'll just be fixing up the man that's getting hung in the morning, but if I can get on the right side of him, he might mix business with pleasure·and give me a letter for when I get out.

PRISONER B. Now we know the cause of all the spring-cleaning.

DUNLAVIN. And a fellow in the kitchen told us they're doing a special dinner for us on account of Uncle Healey's visit.

PRISONER A. Do you mean we're getting food with our meals today?

DUNLAVIN. That's right, and I can't be standing yapping to youse. I've to hang up my holy pictures and think up a few funny remarks for him. God, what Jimmie O'Dea is getting thousands for I've to do for a pair of old socks and a ticket for the Prisoners' Aid.

> DUNLAVIN *goes into his cell. Two* YOUNG PRISONERS *aged about seventeen go past with sweeping brushes in front of them, singing softly and in unison.*

YOUNG PRISONERS.

> Only one more cell inspection
> We go out next Saturday,
> Only one more cell inspection
> And we go far, far away.

PRISONER A. What brings you fellows round here this morning?

YOUNG PRISONER 1. Our screw told us to sweep all round the Juvenile Wing and then to come round here and give it a bit of a going over.

PRISONER B. And have you your own wing done?

YOUNG PRISONER 2. No, but if we did our wing first, we'd miss the mots hanging out the laundry. You can't see them from our wing.

PRISONER A. Just as well, maybe; you're bad enough as it is.

YOUNG PRISONER 1. But I tell you what you will see from our wing this morning. It's the carpenter bringing up the coffin for the quare fellow and leaving it over in the mortuary to have it handy for the morning. There's two orderlies besides us over in the Juveniles, and we were going to toss up who'd come over here, but they're country fellows and they'd said they'd sooner see the coffin. I'd sooner a pike at a good-looking mot than the best coffin in Ireland, wouldn't you, Shaybo?

YOUNG PRISONER 2. Certainly I would, and outside that, when you're over here, there's always a chance of getting a bit of education about screwing jobs, and suchlike, from experienced men. Do you think Triplex or celluloid is the best for Yale locks, sir?

YOUNG PRISONER 1. Do you carry the stick all the time, sir?

PRISONER A. If I had a stick I'd know where to put it, across your bloody . . .

YOUNG PRISONER 2. Scholara, get sweeping, here's the screw.

They drift off sweeping and singing softly.

PRISONER B. He's bringing one of 'em. Is it Silver-top or the other fellow?

PRISONER A. Silver-top. I remember him being half carried into the circle the night he was sentenced to death.

PRISONER B. He has a right spring in his step this morning then.

PRISONER A. He's not looking all that happy. Still, I suppose he hasn't got over the shock yet.

> WARDER *and a* PRISONER *come on* L. *The* PRISONER *is in early middle age; when he speaks he has a "good accent". He is carrying a pillow slip which contains his sheets and other kit. The* WARDER *halts him.*

WARDER REGAN. Stand by the door with your name on it. Later on when you've seen the doctor these fellows will show you how to lay your kit. Stand there now, till the doctor is ready to see you. [*He goes. There is a pause, while the* PRISONERS *survey the newcomer.*]

PRISONER B. He'll bloody well cheer the place up, won't he?

LIFER. Have any of you got a cigarette?

PRISONER A. That's a good one. You're not in the condemned cell now, you know. No snout allowed here.

PRISONER B. Unless you manage to scrounge a dog-end off the remands.

PRISONER A. Or pick one up in the exercise yard after a man the like of yourself that's allowed them as a special concession. Not, by God, that we picked up much after you. What did you do with your dog-ends?

LIFER. Threw them in the fire.

PRISONER B. You what!

PRISONER A. How was it the other poor bastard, that's got no reprieve and is to be topped in the morning—how was it he was always able to leave a trail of butts behind him when he went off exercise?

LIFER. I've never been in prison before; how was I to know?

B

PRISONER A. You're a curse of God liar, my friend, you did know; for it was whispered to him by the fellows from the hospital bringing over the grub to the condemned cell. He never gave them as much as a match! And he couldn't even bring his dog-ends to the exercise yard and drop them behind for us to pick up when we came out later.

PRISONER B. I bet you're charmed with yourself that you're not going through the iron door tomorrow morning.

The LIFER *doesn't speak, but looks down at his suit.*

PRISONER A. Aye, you're better off in that old suit, bad as it is, than the wooden overcoat the quare fellow is going to get tomorrow morning.

PRISONER B. The longest you could do would be twenty years. More than likely you'll get out in half of that. Last man to finish up in the Bog, he done eleven.

LIFER. Eleven. How do you live through it?

PRISONER A. A minute at a time.

PRISONER B. You haven't got a bit of snout for him, have you? [PRISONER A. *shakes his head.*] Maybe Dunlavin has. Hey, Dunlavin, have you e'er a smoke you'd give this chap? Hey, Dunlavin.

DUNLAVIN [*coming from his cell*]. Yes, what is it? Anyone there the name of headache?

PRISONER B. Could you manage to give this chap something to smoke? E'er a bit of snout at all.

DUNLAVIN. There's only one brand of tobacco allowed here—"Three Nuns". None today, none tomorrow, and none the day after.

He goes back into his cell.

PRISONER B. Eh, Dunlavin, come back to hell out of that.

DUNLAVIN. Well, what?

PRISONER B. This poor chap after being smoking about sixty a day . . .

DUNLAVIN. Where?

PRISONER B. In the condemned cell—where else?

DUNLAVIN. Now I have you. Sure I thought you were the other fellow, and you're not, you're only the murderer. God comfort you. [*Shakes hands.*] Certainly so. [*Takes off his jacket, looks up and down the wing, undoes his trousers and from the depths of his combinations he produces a cigarette end, and a match, and presents them to the* LIFER.] Reprieved in the small hours of this morning. Certainly so. The dead arose and appeared to many, as the man said, but you'll be getting yourself a bad name standing near that other fellow's door. This is your flowery dell, see? It has your name there on that little card. And all your particulars. Age forty-three. Religion R.C.

LIFER [*reads*]. Life.

DUNLAVIN. And a bloody sight better than death any day of the week.

PRISONER B. It always says that. The Governor will explain it all to you later this morning.

DUNLAVIN. Or maybe they'll get holy Uncle Healey to do it.

PRISONER B. Go into your cell and have a smoke for yourself. Bring in your kit bag. [*Passes in kit to* LIFER.] Have a quiet burn there before the screw comes round; we'll keep nick. [LIFER *closes the door of his cell.*]

DUNLAVIN. God knows I got the pick of good neighbours. Lovely people. Give me a decent murderer though, rather then the likes of this other fellow. Well, I'll go into me little place and get on with me bit of dobying so as to have it all nice for Healey when he comes round. [He *goes back to his cell.*]

PRISONER B. [*to* LIFER]. Don't light up yet! Here's the screw coming.

PRISONER A. With the other fellow.

> WARDER REGAN *and another prisoner*, "*the* OTHER FELLOW", *an anxious-faced man, wearing prison clothes and carrying a kit bag, come on* L.

WARDER REGAN. Yes, this is your flowery dell. Leave in your kitbag and stand at your door and wait for the doctor. These other fellows will show you where to go when he comes.

OTHER FELLOW. Right, sir. Very good, sir.

> WARDER REGAN *goes, the* OTHER FELLOW *has a look round.*

PRISONER B. There's a bloke in the end cell getting himself a quiet burn. Why don't you join him before the screws get back?

The OTHER FELLOW *notices the card on* LIFER'S *cell.*

OTHER FELLOW. My God! Is this what I've come to, mixing with murderers! I'd rather not, thank you, though I could do with a smoke. I'll have to spend long months here, even if I get my remission, with murderers and thieves and God knows what! You're not all murderers are you? You haven't killed anyone, have you?

PRISONER B. Not for a while, I haven't.

OTHER FELLOW. I cannot imagine any worse crime than taking a life, can you?

PRISONER B. It'd depend whose life.

OTHER FELLOW. Of course. I mean, a murderer would be justified in taking his own life, wouldn't he? "We send him forth" says Carlisle—you've heard of Carlisle haven't you?—"We send him forth, back to the void, back to the darkness, far out beyond the stars. Let him go from us."

DUNLAVIN [*head out of door of cell*]. Oh. [*Looks at* OTHER FELLOW.] I thought it was Healey from the Department or someone giving it out of them.

PRISONER A. Looks like this man is a bit of an intellectual.

DUNLAVIN. Is that what they call it now?

LIFER. Thanks for the smoke, Mr. Dunlavin.

DUNLAVIN. Not at all, sure, you're welcome, call again when you're passing. But remember the next wife you kill and you getting forty fags a day in the condemned cell, think of them as is not so fortunate as yourself and leave a few dog-ends around the exercise yard after you. Here's these noisy little gets again.

The two YOUNG PRISONERS *come round from the left, their sweeping brushes in front of them and singing their song. The* OTHER FELLOW *stands quite still at his door.*

YOUNG PRISONERS.

    Only one more cell inspection
      We go out next Saturday
    Only one more cell inspection
      Then we go far far away.
    [*They are sweeping near the* LIFER.]
    Only one more cell inspection
      We go out next Saturday
    Only one more cell . . .

LIFER. For God's sake shut up that squeaking . . .

YOUNG PRISONER 1. We've as much right to open our mouth as what you have, and you only a wet day in the place.

PRISONER B. Leave the kids alone. You don't own the place, you know. They're doing no harm. [*To the* YOUNG PRISONERS.] You want to sweep this bit of floor away?

DUNLAVIN. What brings you round here so often? If you went over to the remand wings you might pick up a bit of snout or a look at the paper.

YOUNG PRISONER 1. We get a smoke and the *Mail* every day off a limey on our road that's on remand. He's in over the car smuggling. But round here this morning you can see the mots from the laundry over on the female side hanging out the washing in the exercise yard. Do youse look at them? I suppose when you get old, though, you don't much bother about women.

PRISONER B. I'm thirty-six, mac.

YOUNG PRISONER 1. Ah, I thought that. Don't suppose you care if you never see a mot. There's Shaybo there and he never thinks of anything else. Do you think of anything else but women, Shaybo?

YOUNG PRISONER 2. Yes. Robbing and stealing, Scholara. You go to the window and keep an eye out for them and I'll sweep on round here till you give us a call.

YOUNG PRISONER 1. Right, Shaybo, they should be nearly out now. [*Goes up and stands by window.*]

PRISONER B. I forgot about the women.

DUNLAVIN. I didn't. It's a great bit of a treat today—that and having me leg rubbed. Neighbour and I wait in for it.

YOUNG PRISONER 1 [*from the window, in a coarse whisper*]. Shaybo, you can see them now.

YOUNG PRISONER 2. The blondy one from North Crumlin?

YOUNG PRISONER 1. Yes, and there's another one with her. I don't know her.

YOUNG PRISONER 2. Must be a country mot. Scholara doesn't know her. Women.

DUNLAVIN. Women.

PRISONER A. I see the blondy one waving.

YOUNG PRISONER 1. If it's all the one to you, I'd like you to know that's my mot and it's me she's waving at.

PRISONER A. I'll wave you a thick ear.

DUNLAVIN. Hey, Neighbour! Where the hell is he this morning? Neighbour!

AN OLD MAN'S CREAKING VOICE. Here I am, Neighbour, here I am.

> NEIGHBOUR, *a bent old man, comes on from* L., *hobbling as quickly as he can on a stick.*

DUNLAVIN. Ah, you lost mass.

NEIGHBOUR. What, are they gone in already?

DUNLAVIN. No, but they're finished hanging up the top row of clothes. There'll be no stretching or reaching off chairs.

NEIGHBOUR. Still, thanks be to God for small mercies. They'll be out again this day week.

PRISONER A. If you lives to see it.

NEIGHBOUR. Why wouldn't I live to see it as well as what you would? This is not the nearest I was to fine women, nor are they the first good-looking ones I saw.

PRISONER A. With that old cough of yours they could easy be the last.

NEIGHBOUR. God, you're a desperate old gas bag. We remember better-looking women than ever they were, don't we, Dunlavin? Meena La Bloom, do you remember her?

DUNLAVIN. Indeed and I do; many's the seaman myself and Meena gave the hey and a do, and Mickey Finn to.

NEIGHBOUR. And poor May Oblong.

DUNLAVIN. Ah, where do you leave poor May? The Lord have mercy on her, wasn't I with her one night in the digs, and there was a Member of Parliament there, and May after locking him in the back room and taking away his trousers, with him going over the north wall that morning to vote for Home Rule. "For the love of your country and mine," he shouts under the door to May, "give me back me trousers." "So I will," says May, "if you shove a fiver out under the door."

NEIGHBOUR. He had the wad hid? Dirty suspicious old beast.

DUNLAVIN. That's right. He was cute enough to hide his wad somewhere, drunk and all as he was the previous night. All we got in his trousers was a locket of hair of the patriotic plumber of Dolphin's barn that swore to let his hair grow till Ireland was free.

NEIGHBOUR. Ah, poor May, God help her, she was the heart of the roll.

DUNLAVIN. And when she was arrested for carrying on after the curfew, the time of the trouble, she was fined for having concealed about her person two Thompson sub-machine guns, 1921 pattern, three Mills bombs, and a stick of dynamite.

NEIGHBOUR. And will you ever forget poor Lottie L'Es-trange, that got had up for pushing the soldier into Spencer Dock?

DUNLAVIN. Ah, God be with the youth of us.

NEIGHBOUR. And Cork Annie, and Lady Limerick.

DUNLAVIN. And Julia Rice and the Goofy One.

NEIGHBOUR [*turns towards window*]. Hey, you, move out of the way there and give us a look. Dunlavin, come up here before they go, and have a look at the blondy one.

YOUNG PRISONER 1. Go 'long, you dirty old dog. That's my mot you're speaking about. [*Shoves* NEIGHBOUR.] You old heap of dirt, to wave at a decent girl.

PRISONER A. Hey, snots, d'you think you own the bloody place?

YOUNG PRISONER 1. Would you like it, to have that dirty old eyebox looking at your mot?

PRISONER B. He's not going to eat her.

DUNLAVIN [*from behind*]. No, but he'd like to.

YOUNG PRISONER 2. That's right, and Scholara is nearly married to her. At least she had a squealer for him and he has to pay her money every week. Any week he's outside like, to give it, or her to get it.

YOUNG PRISONER 1 [*blows a kiss*]. That's right, and I have him putting his rotten old eye on her.

OTHER FELLOW [*at his doorway*]. God preserve us.

PRISONER A. Well, you don't own the bloody window. [*Shoves* YOUNG PRISONER 1 *out of way and brings over* NEIGHBOUR.] Come on, you, if you want to see the May procession.

NEIGHBOUR. Ah, thanks, butty, your blood's worth bottling.

PRISONER A. I didn't do it on account of you, but if you let them young pups get away with too much they'd be running the place.

YOUNG PRISONER 2. Come on, Scholara, we'll mosey back. The screw will think we're lost.

They go back down the stairs, pick up their brushes, and start sweeping again and singing . . .

YOUNG PRISONER 1.

> Only one more cell inspection
> We go out next Saturday

YOUNG PRISONER 2.

> Only one more cell inspection . . .

LIFER. Shut your bloody row, can't you?

DUNLAVIN. Shut up yourself; you're making more noise than any of them.

YOUNG PRISONER 1. Don't tell us to shut up, you bastard.

PRISONER B. Ah leave him alone; he started life this morning.

YOUNG PRISONER 1. Ah we're sorry, mister, ain't we, Shaybo?

YOUNG PRISONER 2. God, we are. Go over and take a pike at the female yard. They hang up the clothes now and Scholara's mot is over there. You can have a look at her. Scholara won't mind, will you, Schol?

YOUNG PRISONER 1. Certainly and I won't. Not with you going to the Bog to start life in a couple of days, where you won't see a woman.

YOUNG PRISONER 2. A child.

YOUNG PRISONER 1. A dog.

YOUNG PRISONER 2. A fire.

PRISONER A. Get to hell out of that round to your own wing. Wouldn't you think a man would know all that forbye you telling it to him?

YOUNG PRISONER 2. We were going anyway. We've seen all we wanted to see. It wasn't to look at a lot of old men we came here, but to see mots hanging out the washing.

YOUNG PRISONER 1. And eitherways, we'll be a lot nearer the women than you'll be next Saturday night. Think of us when you're sitting locked up in the old flowery, studying the Bible, Chapter 1, verse 2, and we trucking round in chase of charver.

They samba out with their brushes for partners, humming the Wedding Samba.

PRISONER A. Them young gets have too much old gab out of them altogether. I was a Y.P. in Walton before the war and I can tell you they'd be quiet boys if they got the larrying we used to get.

OTHER FELLOW. And talking so disrespectfully about the Bible.

NEIGHBOUR. Belied and they needn't; many's the time the Bible was a consolation to a fellow all alone in the old cell. The lovely thin paper with a bit of mattress coir in it, if you could get a match or a bit of tinder or any class of light, was as good a smoke as ever I tasted. Am I right, Dunlavin?

DUNLAVIN. Damn the lie, Neighbour. The first twelve months I done, I smoked my way half-way through the book of Genesis and three inches of my mattress. When the Free State came in we were afraid of our life they were going to change the mattresses for feather beds. And you couldn't smoke feathers, not, be God, if they were rolled in the Song of Solomon itself. But sure, thanks to God, the Free State didn't change anything more than the badge on the warders' caps.

OTHER FELLOW. Can I be into my cell for a while?

PRISONER B. Until the doctor calls you. [*Goes into his cell.*]

PRISONER A. Well, I'm going to have a rest. It's hard work doing a lagging.

LIFER. A lagging? That's penal servitude, isn't it?

DUNLAVIN. Three years or anything over.

LIFER. Three years is a long time.

DUNLAVIN. I wouldn't like to be that long hanging.

NEIGHBOUR. Is he the . . .

DUNLAVIN [*sotto voce*]. Silver-top! [*Aloud.*] Started life this morning.

NEIGHBOUR. So they're not going to top you after all? Well, you're a lucky man. I worked one time in the hospital, helping the screw there, and the morning of the execution he gave me two bottles of stout to take the hood off the fellow was after being topped. I wouldn't have done it a second time for two glasses of malt, no, nor a bottle of it. I cut the hood away; his head was all twisted and his face black, but the two eyes were the worst; like a rabbit's; it was fear that had done it.

LIFER. Perhaps he didn't feel anything. How do you know?

NEIGHBOUR. I only seen him. I never had a chance of asking him. [NEIGHBOUR *goes to the murderer's door.*] Date of expiration of sentence, life. In some ways I wouldn't mind if that was my lot. What do you say?

DUNLAVIN. I don't know; it's true we're too old and bet for lobbywatching and shaking down anywhere, so that you'd fall down and sleep on the pavement of a winter's night and not know but you were lying snug and comfortable in the Shelbourne.

NEIGHBOUR. Only then to wake up on some lobby and the hard floorboards under you, and a lump of hard filth for your pillow, and the cold and the drink shaking you, wishing it was morning for the market pubs to open, where if you had the price of a drink you could sit in the warm anyway. Except, God look down on you, if it was Sunday.

DUNLAVIN. Ah, there's the agony. No pub open, but the bells battering your bared nerves and all you could do with the cold and the sickness was to lean over on your side and wish that God would call you.

LIFER. If I was outside my life wouldn't be like that.

NEIGHBOUR. No, but ours would.

DUNLAVIN [quietly]. See, we're selfish, mister, like everyone else.

WARDER [shouts off]. Medical applications and receptions. Fall in for the doctor. [LIFER looks lost.]

DUNLAVIN. Yes, that's you. Go up there to the top of the wing and wait there till the screw tells you to go in. Neighbour, call them other fellows.

    Exit LIFER.

NEIGHBOUR. Come on—the vet's here.

DUNLAVIN [calling in to the OTHER FELLOW]. Hey, come out and get gelded.

    OTHER FELLOW and PRISONERS A. and B. come out of cells.

NEIGHBOUR. You're for the doctor. Go on up there with the rest of them. Me and Dunlavin don't go up. We only wait to be rubbed.

DUNLAVIN. Don't have any chat at all with that fellow. D'you see what he's in for?

NEIGHBOUR *goes and looks. Exit* OTHER FELLOW *and* PRISONERS A. *and* B.

NEIGHBOUR. What the hell does that mean?

DUNLAVIN. A bloody sex mechanic.

NEIGHBOUR. I didn't know.

DUNLAVIN. Well, you know now. I'll go in and get me chair. You can sit on it after me. It'll save you bringing yours out.

NEIGHBOUR. Well, if you go first and you have a chance of a go at the spirit bottle, don't swig the bloody lot. Remember I'm for treatment too.

DUNLAVIN. Don't be such an old begrudger. He'll bring a quart bottle of it, and who could swallow that much methylated spirit in the few drops you'd get at it?

NEIGHBOUR. You could, or a bucket of it, if it was lying anywhere handy. I seen you do it, bluestone and all, only buns to a bear as far as you were concerned.

DUNLAVIN. Do you remember the old doctor they had here years ago?

NEIGHBOUR. The one they used to call Crippen.

DUNLAVIN. The very man. There was one day I was brought in for drinking the chat and I went to court that morning and was here in the afternoon still as drunk as Pontius Pilate. Crippen was examining me. "When I put me hand there you cough," and all to that effect. "Did you ever have V.D.?" says he. "I haven't got your habits," says I to him. These fellows weren't long.

Re-enter PRISONERS A. *and* B.

NEIGHBOUR. What did he give youse?

PRISONER B. [*passing into cell*]. Extra six ounces of bread. Says we're undernourished.

PRISONER A. Is the bar open yet?

NEIGHBOUR. Never you mind the bar. I've cruel pains in my leg that I want rubbed to take out the rheumatics, not to be jeered at, and I've had them genuine since the war.

PRISONER A. What war? The economic war?

NEIGHBOUR. Ah, you maggot. It's all your fault, Dunlavin, telling them fellows we do get an odd sup out of the spirit bottle. Letting everyone know our business.

PRISONERS A. *and* B. *go into cells and shut the doors.*

DUNLAVIN. No sign of Holy Healey yet.

NEIGHBOUR. You're wasting your time chasing after old Healey. He told me here one day, and I trying to get myself an old overcoat out of him, that he was here only as a head man of the Department of Justice, and he couldn't do other business of any other sort or size whatever, good, bad or indifferent. It's my opinion that old Healey does be half-jarred a deal of the time anyway.

DUNLAVIN. The likes of Healey would take a sup all right, but being a high-up civil servant, he wouldn't drink under his own name. You'd see the likes of Healey nourishing themselves with balls of malt, at eleven in the morning, in little back snugs round Merrion Row. The barman would lose his job if he so much as breathed their name. It'd be "Mr. H. wants a drop of water but not too much." "Yes, Mr. O." "No, sir, Mr. Mac wasn't in this morning." "Yes, Mr. D. Fine morning; it will be a lovely day if it doesn't snow." Educated drinking, you know. Even a bit of chat about God at an odd time, so as you'd think God was in another department, but not long off the Bog, and they was doing Him a good turn to be talking well about Him.

NEIGHBOUR. Here's the other two back. The M.O. will be down to us soon.

>   LIFER *and* OTHER FELLOW *go into cells and shut the doors.*

DUNLAVIN. That other fellow's not looking as if this place is agreeing with him.

NEIGHBOUR. You told me a minute ago that I wasn't even to speak to him.

DUNLAVIN. Ah, when all is said and done, he's someone's rearing after all, he could be worse, he could be a screw or an official from the Department.

>   WARDER REGAN *comes on with a bottle marked "methy-lated spirit".*

WARDER REGAN. You're the two for rubs, for your rheumatism.

DUNLAVIN. That's right, Mr. Regan sir, old and bet, sir, that's us. And the old pains is very bad with us these times, sir.

WARDER REGAN. Not so much lip, and sit down whoever is first for treatment.

DUNLAVIN. That's me, sir. Age before ignorance, as the man said. [*Sits in the chair.*]

WARDER REGAN. Rise the leg of your trousers. Which leg is it?

DUNLAVIN. The left, sir.

WARDER REGAN. That's the right leg you're showing me.

DUNLAVIN. That's what I was saying, sir. The left is worst one day and the right is bad the next. To be on the safe side, you'd have to do two of them. It's only the mercy of God I'm not a centipede, sir, with the weather that's in it.

WARDER REGAN. Is that where the pain is?

DUNLAVIN [*bending down slowly towards the bottle*]. A little lower down, sir, if you please. [*Grabs the bottle and raises it to his mouth.*] Just a little lower down, sir, if it's all equal to you.

> REGAN *rubs, head well bent, and* DUNLAVIN *drinks long and deeply and as quickly lowers the bottle on to the floor again, wiping his mouth and making the most frightful grimaces, for the stuff doesn't go down easy at first. He goes through the pantomime of being burnt inside for* NEIGHBOUR'S *benefit and rubs his mouth with the back of his hand.*

DUNLAVIN. Ah, that's massive, sir. 'Tis you that has the healing hand. You must have desperate luck at the horses; I'd only love to be with you copying your dockets. [REGAN *turns and pours more spirit on his hands.*] Ah, that's it, sir, well into me I can feel it going. [*Reaches forward towards the bottle again, drinks.*] Ah, that's it, I can feel it going right into me. And doing me all the good in the world. [REGAN *reaches and puts more spirit on his hand and sets to rubbing again.*] That's it, sir, thorough does it; if you're going to do a thing at all you might as well do it well. [*Reaches forward for the bottle again and raises it.* NEIGHBOUR *looks across in piteous appeal to him not to drink so much, but he merely waves the bottle in elegant salute, as if to wish him good health, and takes another drink.*] May God reward you, sir, you must be the seventh son of the seventh son or one of the Lees from Limerick on your mother's side maybe. [*Drinks again.*] Ah, that's the cure for the cold of the wind and the world's neglectment.

WARDER REGAN. Right, now you.

C

NEIGHBOUR *comes forward.*

WARDER DONELLY (*offstage*). All present and correct, Mr. Healey, sir.

DUNLAVIN. Holy Healey!

Enter WARDER DONELLY.

WARDER DONELLY. This way, Mr. Healey.

WARDER REGAN. Attention! Stand by your doors.

DUNLAVIN. By the left, laugh.

WARDER DONELLY. This way.

Enter MR. HEALEY, *an elegantly dressed gentleman.*

HEALEY. Good morning.

WARDER DONELLY. Any complaints?

PRISONER A. No, sir.

HEALEY. Good morning!

WARDER DONELLY. Any complaints?

OTHER FELLOW. ⎫
PRISONER B.   ⎭ No, sir.

HEALEY. Good morning all! Well, now, I'm here representing the Department of Justice, if there are any complaints now is the time to make them.

SEVERAL PRISONERS. No complaints, sir.

WARDEN REGAN. All correct, sir. Two receiving medical treatment here, sir.

DUNLAVIN. Just getting the old leg rubbed, sir, Mr. Healey.

HEALEY. Well, well, it almost smells like a bar.

DUNLAVIN. I'm near drunk myself on the smell of it, sir.

HEALEY. Don't let me interrupt the good work.

DUNLAVIN. Ah, the old legs. It's being out in all weathers that does it, sir. Of course we don't have that to contend with while we're here, sir.

HEALEY. Out in all weathers, I should think not indeed. Well, my man, I will be inspecting your cell amongst others in due course.

DUNLAVIN. Yes, sir.

HEALEY. It's always a credit to you, I must say that. [*He turns to* REGAN.] Incorrigible, some of these old fellows, but rather amusing.

WARDER REGAN. Yes, sir.

HEALEY. It's Regan, isn't it?

WARDER REGAN. Yes, sir.

HEALEY. Ah yes, you're helping the Canon at the execution tomorrow morning, I understand.

WARDER REGAN. Well, I shall be with the condemned man sir, seeing that he doesn't do away with himself during the night and that he goes down the hole with his neck properly broken in the morning, without making too much fuss about it.

HEALEY. A sad duty.

WARDER REGAN. Neck breaking and throttling, sir? [HEALEY *gives him a sharp look*.] You must excuse me, sir. I've seen rather a lot of it. They say familiarity breeds contempt.

HEALEY. Well, we have one consolation, Regan, the condemned man gets the priest and the sacraments, more than his victim got maybe. I venture to suggest that some of them die holier deaths than if they had finished their natural span.

WARDER REGAN. We can't advertise "Commit a murder and die a happy death," sir. We'd have them all at it. They take religion very seriously in this country.

HEALEY. Quite, quite so! Now, I understand you have the reprieved man over here, Regan.

WARDER REGAN. No. twenty-six sir.

DUNLAVIN. Just beside me, sir.

HEALEY. Ah, yes! So here we are! Here's the lucky man,
eh? Well, now, the Governor will explain your position
to you later in the day. Your case will be examined every
five years. Meanwhile I thought you might like a holy
picture to hang up in your cell. Keep a cheerful coun-
tenance, my friend. God gave you back your life and the
least you can do is to thank him with every breath you
draw! Right? Well, be of good heart. I will call in and
see you again, that is, if duty permits. [He *moves to*
DUNLAVIN'S *cell*.]

HEALEY [*at* DUNLAVIN'S *cell*]. Very creditable. Hm.

DUNLAVIN. Well, to tell you the truth, sir, it's a bit extra
special today. You see, we heard you was here.

HEALEY. Very nice.

DUNLAVIN. Of course I do like to keep my little place as
homely as I can with the little holy pictures you gave me
of Blessed Martin, sir.

HEALEY. I see you don't recognize the colour bar.

DUNLAVIN. The only bar I recognize, sir, is the Bridge Bar
or the Beamish House the corner of Thomas Street.

HEALEY. Well, I must be off now, and I'm glad to see you're
being well looked after.

DUNLAVIN. It's neither this nor that, but if you could spare
a minute, sir?

HEALEY. Yes, what is it? But hurry; remember I've a lot to
do today.

DUNLAVIN. It's like this, sir. I won't always be here, sir,
having me leg rubbed and me bit of grub brought to me.

As it says in the Bible, sir, have it yourself or be without it and put ye by for the rainy day, for thou knowest not the night thou mayest be sleeping in a lobby.

HEALEY. Yes, yes, but what is it you want?

DUNLAVIN. I've the chance of a little room up round Buckingham Street, sir, if you could only give me a letter to the Room-Keepers after I go out, for a bit of help with the rent.

HEALEY. Well, you know, when I visit the prison, I'm not here as a member of any outside organization of which I may be a member but simply as an official of the Department of Justice.

DUNLAVIN. Yes, but where else would I be likely to meet you, sir? I'd hardly bump into you in the Bridge Bar when I'd be outside, would I, sir?

HEALEY. No, no, certainly not. But you know the Society offices in the Square. See me there any Friday night, between eight and nine.

DUNLAVIN. Thank you, sir, and a bed in heaven to you, sir.

HEALEY. And the same to you. [*Goes to next cell.*]

DUNLAVIN. And many of them, and I hope we're all here this time next year [*venomously after* MR. HEALEY] that it may choke you.

> WARDER DONELLY *bangs on* LIFER'S *closed door, then looks in.*

WARDER DONELLY. Jesus Christ, sir. He's put the sheet up! Quick.

> REGAN *and* DONELLY *go into* LIFER'S *cell. He is hanging. They cut him down.*

WARDER REGAN. Gently does it.

They lay him down in the passage and try to restore him.

HEALEY. What a dreadful business, and with this other coming off tomorrow.

THE PRISONERS *crowd out of line.*

WARDER DONELLY. Get back to your cells!

HEALEY. Is he still with us?

WARDER REGAN. He'll be all right in an hour or two. Better get the M.O., Mr. Donelly.

The triangle sounds.

WARDER DONELLY. B. Wing, two, three and one. Stand by your doors. Right, lead on. Now come on, come on, this is no holiday. Right sir, over to you. Lead on, B.1.

WARDER REGAN *and* HEALEY *are left with the unconscious* LIFER.

HEALEY. Dear, dear. The Canon will be very upset about this.

WARDER REGAN. There's not much harm done, thank God. They don't have to put a death certificate against the receipt for his live body.

HEALEY. That doesn't seem a very nice way of looking at it, Regan.

WARDER REGAN. A lot of people mightn't consider ours a very nice job, sir.

HEALEY. Ours?

WARDER REGAN. Yes, ours, sir. Mine, the Canon's, the hangman's, and if you don't mind my saying so, yours, sir.

HEALEY. Society cannot exist without prisons, Regan. My

job is to bring what help and comfort I can to these un-
fortunates. Really, a man with your outlook, I cannot see
why you stay in the service.

WARDER REGAN. It's a soft job, sir, between hangings.

The triangle is heard. The M.O. *comes on with two stretcher-
bearers.*

The curtain falls.

ACT II

The curtain rises

The prison yard, a fine evening.

VOICE OF PRISONER [*off-stage, singing*].

> A hungry feeling came o'er me stealing
> And the mice were squealing in my prison cell
> And the old triangle
> Went jingle jangle
> Along the banks of the Royal Canal.

WARDER DONELLY. B.1. B.2. B.3. Head on for exercise, right! Lead on, B.1. All one, away to exercise.

The prisoners file out, WARDER DONELLY *with them.*

> On a fine spring evening,
> The lag lay dreaming
> The seagulls wheeling high above the wall,
> And the old triangle
> Went jingle jangle
> Along the banks of the Royal Canal.
> The screw was peeping
> The lag was sleeping,

The prisoners wander where they will; most go and take a glance at the half-dug grave.

> While he lay weeping for the girl Sal,

WARDER DONELLY. Who's the bloody baritone? Shut up that noise, you. Where do you think you are?

NEIGHBOUR. It's not up here, sir; it's one of the fellows in the basement, sir, in the solitary.

WARDER DONELLY. He must be getting birdseed with his bread and water. I'll bloody well show him he's not in a singing house. [*Song is still going on.*] Hey, shut up that noise! Shut up there or I'll leave you weeping. Where do you think you are? [*Song stops.*] You can get sitting down any of you that wants it. [DUNLAVIN *sits.*]

NEIGHBOUR [*at the grave*]. They'll have to bottom out another couple of feet before morning.

PRISONER B. They! Us you mean; they've got four of us in a working party after tea.

NEIGHBOUR. You want to get that clay nice and neat for filling in. [*He spits and wanders away.*]

PRISONER B. We'll get a couple of smokes for the job at least.

   They wander.

NEIGHBOUR. How are you, Neighbour?

DUNLAVIN. Dying.

NEIGHBOUR. If you are itself, it's greed that's killing you. I only got a sup of what was left.

DUNLAVIN. I saved your life then; it was very bad meths.

PRISONER B. What did Regan say when he caught youse lying in the cell?

NEIGHBOUR. He wanted to take us up for drinking it on him, but Dunlavin said we were distracted with the events of the morning and didn't know what we were doing. So he just told us to get to hell out of it and he hoped it would destroy us for life.

DUNLAVIN. May God forgive him.

NEIGHBOUR. I thought it was as good a drop of meths as ever I tasted. It would never come up to the pre-war article, but between the spring-time and the warmth of it, it would put new life into you. Oh, it's a grand evening and another day's work behind us.

PRISONER B. With the winter over, Neighbour, I suppose you don't feel a day over ninety.

NEIGHBOUR. If you'd have done all the time I have you wouldn't look so young.

PRISONER A. What time? Sure, you never done a lagging in your life. A month here and a week there for lifting the collection box out of a chapel or running out of a chemist's with a bottle of cheap wine. Anything over six months would be the death of you.

NEIGHBOUR. Oh, you're the hard chaw.

PRISONER A. Two laggings, I've done. Five year and seven, and a bit of Preventive Detention, on the Moor and at Parkhurst.

NEIGHBOUR. What for? Ferocious begging?

PRISONER A. I've never been a grasshopper or a nark for the screws anyway, wherever I was; and if you were in a lagging station I know what they'd give you, shopping the poor bastard that was singing in the chokey. He was only trying to be company for himself down there all alone and not knowing whether it was day or night.

NEIGHBOUR. I only did it for his own good. If the screw hadn't checked him the Principal might have been coming out and giving him an extra few days down there.

DUNLAVIN. Will youse give over the pair of youse for God's sake. The noise of youse battering me bared nerves is unhuman. Begod, an Englishman would have more nature to a fellow lying with a sick head. A methylated martyr, that's what I am.

NEIGHBOUR [*to* PRISONER A.]. Meself and that man sitting there, we done time before you came up. In Kilmainham, and that's where you never were. First fourteen days without a mattress, skilly three times a day. None of your sitting out in the yard like nowadays. I got my toe amputated by one of the old lags so I could get into hospital for a feed.

DUNLAVIN [*looks up and feebly moans*]. A pity you didn't get your head amputated as you were at it. It would have kept you quiet for a bit.

NEIGHBOUR. I got me mouth to talk, the same as the next man. Maybe we're not all that well up, that we get up at the Christmas concert and do the electrocutionist performance, like some I could mention.

DUNLAVIN. It's neither this nor that, Neighbour, but if you would only give over arguing the toss about nothing and change over to a friendly subject of mutual interest— like the quare fellow that's to be topped in the morning.

NEIGHBOUR. True, true, Dunlavin, and a comfortable old flowery dell he'll have down there. (He *prods the grave with his stick.*] We'll be eating the cabbages off that one in a month or two.

PRISONER A. You're in a terrible hurry to get the poor scut under the cabbages. How do you know he won't get a reprieve, like old Silver-top?

LIFER. Jesus, Mary and Joseph, you'd like to see me in there, wouldn't you! [*He moves violently away from them.*]

NEIGHBOUR. Your man doesn't like any talk about hanging.

PRISONER A. No more would you, if you'd tried to top yourself this morning.

NEIGHBOUR. Anyway he's gone now and we can have a chat about it in peace. Sure we must be saying something and it's better than scandalizing our neighbours.

PRISONER B. You never know what might happen to the quare fellow. God is good.

PRISONER C. And has a good mother.

> *They look in surprise at the young person who has quietly joined them.*

DUNLAVIN. No, no, it's too late now for him to be chucked.

PRISONER A. It has been known, a last-minute reprieve, you know.

NEIGHBOUR. He bled his brother into a crock, didn't he, that had been set aside for the pig-slaughtering and mangled the remains beyond all hope of identification.

PRISONER C. Go bfoiridh Dia reinn.

NEIGHBOUR. He hasn't got a chance, never in a race of cats. He'll be hung as high as Guilderoy.

PRISONER A. You're the life of the party, aren't you? You put me in mind of the little girl who was sent in to cheer her father up. She was so good at it that he cut his throat.

PRISONER E. Ah, sure he was only computing the odds to it. He'll be topped.

NEIGHBOUR. I'd lay me Sunday bacon on it if anyone would be idiot enough to take me up.

> PRISONER E, *a bookie, has been listening.*

PRISONER E. I wouldn't take your bacon, but I'll lay it off for you if you like.

> *Another prisoner watches for the screws.* PRISONER E. *acts as if he were a tick-tack man at the races.*

PRISONER E. The old firm. Here we are again. Neighbour lays his Sunday bacon the quare fellow will be topped tomorrow morning. Any takers?

PRISONER D. Five snout.

PRISONER E. Away home to your mother.

MICKSER. Half a bacon.

PRISONER E. Half a . . .

NEIGHBOUR. Even bacons.

PRISONER E. Even bacons. Even bacons any takers? Yourself, sir, come on now, you look like a sportsman.

PRISONER A. I wouldn't eat anything after he'd touched it, not if I were starving.

NEIGHBOUR. Is that so . . .

PRISONER E. Now, now, now, don't interrupt the betting. Any takers?

DUNLAVIN. I'll take him up if only to shut his greedy gob.

NEIGHBOUR. You won't! You're having me on!

DUNLAVIN. No, I'll bet you my Sunday bacon that a reprieve will come through before morning. I feel it in my bones.

NEIGHBOUR. That's the rheumatics.

PRISONER E. Is he on, Neighbour?

NEIGHBOUR. He is.

PRISONER E. Shake on it, the two of youse!

DUNLAVIN. How d'ye do, Lord Lonsdale!

NEIGHBOUR. Never mind all that. The minute the trap goes down tomorrow morning your Sunday bacon is mine.

PRISONER A. God leave you health to enjoy it.

NEIGHBOUR. He'll be topped all right.

PRISONER A. And if he isn't, I'm the very man will tell him you bet your bacon on his life.

NEIGHBOUR. You never would.

PRISONER A. Wouldn't I?

NEIGHBOUR. You'd never be bad enough.

PRISONER A. And what would be bad about it?

NEIGHBOUR. Causing a dissension and a disturbance.

The two YOUNG PRISONERS *enter.*

PRISONER A. You mean he mightn't take it for a joke.

PRISONER B. Here's them two young prisoners; they've the life of Reilly, rambling round the place. Where youse wandering off to now?

SCHOLARA. We came over here to see a chiner of ours. He turned twenty the day before yesterday, so they shifted him away from the Juveniles to here. [*He sees* PRISONER C.] Ah, there you are. We were over in the hospital being examined for going out on Saturday and we had a bit of snout to give you. [*Takes out a Woodbine package, extracts a cigarette from it and gives it to* PRISONER C., *who shyly stands and takes it.*]

PRISONER C. [*quietly*]. Thanks.

SCHOLARA. Gurra morra gut, you mean.

PRISONER C. [*smiles faintly*]. Go raibh maith agat.

SCHOLARA [*grandly*]. Na bac leis. [*To the other prisoners.*] Talks Irish to beat the band. Comes from an island between here and America. And Shaybo will give you a couple of strikers.

SHAYBO [*reaches in the seams of his coat and takes out a match which he presents to* PRISONER C.]. Here you are. It's a bloody shame to shove you over here among all these old men even if you are twenty itself, but maybe you won't be long after us, and you going home.

PRISONER C. [*Kerry accent*]. I will, please God. It will be summer-time and where I come from is lovely when the sun is shining.

[*They stand there, looking embarrassed for a moment.*]

DUNLAVIN. Go on, why don't you kiss him good-bye.

SHAYBO. Eh, Schol, let's have a pike at the grave before the screw comes out.

SCHOLARA. Ah, yes, we must have a look at the grave.

They dive into the grave, the old men shout at them, but WARDER DONELLY *comes to the door of the hospital.*

WARDER DONELLY. Get up to hell out of that and back to your own wing, youse two. [*Shouts to the warders in the prison wing.*] Two on you there, pass them fellows into the Juveniles. Get to hell out of that!

SCHOLARA *and* SHAYBO *samba off, give the so-called V-sign, slap the right biceps with the left palm, and turning lightly, run in through the door.*

NEIGHBOUR. Aren't they the impudent pups? Too easy a time they have of it. I'd tan their pink backsides for them. That'd leave them fresh and easy. Impudent young curs is going these days. No respect for God nor man, pinch anything that wasn't nailed down.

PRISONER B. Neighbour, the meths is rising in you.

DUNLAVIN. He might as well rave there as in bed.

ENGLISH VOICE [*from one of the cell windows*]. I say, I say, down there in the yard.

DUNLAVIN. The voice of the Lord!

PRISONER A. That's the geezer from London that's in over the car smuggling.

ENGLISH VOICE. I say, down there.

PRISONER B. Hello, up there.

NEIGHBOUR. How are you fixed for fillet?

PRISONER B. Shut up a minute. Wait till we hear what is it he wants.

ENGLISH VOICE. Is there any bloke down there going out this week?

PRISONER B. Mickser is going out tomorrow. He's on this exercise. [*Shouts.*] Hold on a minute. [*Looks round.*] Hey, Mickser.

MICKSER. What's up?

PRISONER B. That English fellow that's on remand over the cars, he wants to know if there's anyone going out this week. You're going out tomorrow, ain't you?

MICKSER. Yes, I am. I'm going out in the morning. [*To* ENGLISH PRISONER.] What do you want?

ENGLISH VOICE. I want you to go up and contact my mate. He's in Dublin. It's about bail for me. I can write his name and address here and let it down to you on my string. I didn't want the law to get his address in Dublin, so I can't write to him. I got a quid in with me, without the screw finding it, and I'll let it down with the address if you'll do it.

MICKSER. Good enough. Let down the address and the quid.

ENGLISH VOICE. My mate will give you some more when you see him.

MICKSER. That's all right. Let the quid down now and the address before the screw comes out of the hospital. I'm going out tomorrow and I'll see him for you, soon as we get out of the market pubs at half two.

PRISONER B. He's letting it down now.

MICKSER. There's the quid anyway. [*Reading the note.* NEIGHBOUR *gets to his feet and goes behind and peers over his shoulder.* MICKSER *sees him.*] Get to hell out of it, you.

NEIGHBOUR. I only just wanted to have a look at what he wrote.

MICKSER. And have his mate in the Bridewell, before the day was out. I know you, you bloody old stag.

NEIGHBOUR. I saw the day you wouldn't say the like of that.

MICKSER [*proffering him the pound*]. Here, get a mass said for yourself.

NEIGHBOUR. It wouldn't do you much harm to put yourself under the hand of a priest either.

MICKSER [*laughs at him*]. That's for sinners. Only dirty people has to wash.

NEIGHBOUR. A man of your talent and wasting your time here.

MICKSER [*going back to walk with the prisoners behind*]. Good luck now, Neighbour. I'll call up and see you in the hospice for the dying.

NEIGHBOUR [*stands and calls loudly after him*]. You watch yourself. I saw the quare fellow in here a couple of years ago. He was a young hard chaw like you in all the pride of his strength and impudence. He was kicking a ball about over in A yard and I was walking around with poor old Mockridge, neither of us minding no one. All of a sudden I gets such a wallop on the head it knocks the legs from under me and very nigh cuts off my ear. "You

D

headed that well", says he, and I deaf for three days after it! Who's got the best of it now, young as he is and strong as he is? How will his own ear feel tomorrow morning, with the washer under it, and whose legs will be the weakest when the trap goes down and he's slung into the pit? And what use is the young heart?

> *Some of the prisoners walking round stop and listen to him, but* MICKSER *gives him a contemptuous look and walks on, shouting at him in passing.*

MICKSER. Get along with you, you dirty half animal.

> *A* WARDER *passes, sounds of the town heard, factory sirens, distant ships. Some of the prisoners pace up and down like caged animals.*

NEIGHBOUR. Dunlavin, have you the loan of a pencil for a minute?

DUNLAVIN. What do you want it for?

NEIGHBOUR. I just want to write something to that English fellow about his bail.

DUNLAVIN. You'd better hurry, before the screw comes back out.

> NEIGHBOUR *writes.*

NEIGHBOUR. Hey, you up there that's looking for the bail.

ENGLISH VOICE. Hello, you got the quid and the address?

PRISONER A. What's the old dog up to?

DUNLAVIN. Ah, leave him alone. He's a bit hasty, but poor old Neighbour has good turns in him.

PRISONER A. So has a corkscrew.

NEIGHBOUR. Let down your string and I'll send you up this bit of a message.

ENGLISH VOICE [*his hands can be seen at the window holding the note*]. "Get a bucket and bail yourself out." [*Shouts in rage.*] You dirty bastard bleeder to take my quid and I'll tell the bloody screw I will; I'll shop you, you bleeding . . .

MICKSER. What's up with you?

NEIGHBOUR. Get a bucket and bail yourself out. [*Laughing an old man's cackle.*]

ENGLISH VOICE. You told me to get a bucket and bail my bleeding self out, but I'll tell the screw; I'll shop you about that quid.

MICKSER [*shouts up to the window*] Shut your bloody big mouth for a minute. I told you nothing.

PRISONER A. It was this old get here.

MICKSER. I sent you no message; it was this old pox bottle.

NEIGHBOUR [*ceases to laugh, is alarmed at the approach of* MICKSER]. Now, now, Mickser, take a joke, can't you, it was only a bit of gas.

MICKSER [*advancing*]. I'll give you gas.

(MICKSER *advances on* NEIGHBOUR. *The lags stop and look—suddenly* MICKSER *seizes the old man and, yelling with delight, carries* NEIGHBOUR *over to the grave and thrusts him into it. The prisoners all crowd around kicking dirt on to the old man and shouting "Get a bucket and bail yourself out".*

PRISONER B. Nick, Mickser, nick, nick here's the screw.

PRISONER A. It's only the cook with the quare fellow's tea.

A PRISONER *comes through the hospital gate and down the steps. He wears a white apron, carries a tray and is surrounded by an interested band, except for the* LIFER, *who stands apart, and* DUNLAVIN, *who lies prone on the front asleep. From the prisoners around the food rises an excited chorus:*

PRISONER A. Rashers and eggs.

PRISONER B. He got that last night.

MICKSER. Chicken.

NEIGHBOUR. He had that for dinner.

PRISONER B. Sweet cake.

PRISONER A. It's getting hung he is, not married.

NEIGHBOUR. Steak and onions.

MICKSER. Sausages and bacon.

PRISONER B. And liver.

PRISONER A. Pork chops.

PRISONER B. Pig's feet.

PRISONER A. Salmon.

NEIGHBOUR. Fish and chips.

MICKSER. Jelly and custard.

NEIGHBOUR. Roast lamb.

PRISONER A. Plum pudding.

PRISONER B. Turkey.

NEIGHBOUR. Goose.

PRISONERS A., B., AND NEIGHBOUR. Rashers and eggs.

ALL. Rashers and eggs, rashers and eggs, and eggs and rashers and eggs and rashers it is.

COOK [*desperate*]. Ah, here, lads.

PRISONERS. Here, give us a look, lift up the lid, eh, here, I never seen it.

> The COOK *struggles to protect his cargo, the* PRISONERS *mill round in a loose scrum of excitement and greed, their nostrils mad almost to the point of snatching a bit. There is a roar from the gate.*

WARDER DONELLY [*from inside the hospital gate*]. Get to hell out of that. What do youse think you are on?

The PRISONERS *scatter in a rush.*

The COOK *with great dignity carries on.*

NEIGHBOUR [*sitting down*]. Oh, the two eggs, the yolk in the middle like . . . a bride's eye under a pink veil, and the grease of the rashers . . . pale and pure like melted gold.

DUNLAVIN. Oh, may God forgive you, as if a body wasn't sick enough as it is.

NEIGHBOUR. And the two big back rashers.

PRISONER A. Go along, you begrudging old dog. Maybe when you go back the standard of living in your town residence, No. 1 St. James Street, might be gone up. And they'll be serving rashers and eggs. You'd do a lot for them, when you'd begrudge them to a man for his last meal on this earth.

NEIGHBOUR. Well, it's not his last meal if you want to know. He'll get a supper tonight and a breakfast in the morning, and I don't begrudge him the little he'll eat of that, seeing the rope stew to follow, and lever pudding and trap door doddle for desert. And anyway didn't you run over the same as the rest of us to see what he was getting?

PRISONER A. And if I did, it wasn't to begrudge it to the man.

PRISONER B. Sure we all ran over, anything to break the monotony in a kip like this.

The triangle is heard.

PRISONER A. [*gloomily*]. I suppose you're right. In Strangeways, Manchester, and I in it during the war, we used to wish for an air-raid. We had one and we were left locked up in our cells. We stood up on our tables and took the blackouts off the windows and had a grand-stand view of the whole city burning away under us. The screws were running round shouting in the spy-holes at us to get down from the windows, but they soon ran off down the shelters. We had a great view of the whole thing till a bomb landed on the Assize Court next door, and the blast killed twenty of the lags. They were left standing on their tables without a mark on them, stone dead. Sure anyway, we all agreed it broke the monotony.

Enter WARDER DONELLY.

WARDER DONELLY. Right, fall in there!

PRISONER B. Don't forget the bet, Neighbour.

WARDER DONELLY. Come on, get in line there.

PRISONER A. And don't forget what I'm going to tell the quare fellow.

WARDER DONELLY. Silence there. [*Search begins.*] What's this you've got in your pocket? A file? Scissors out of the bag shop? No? A bit of rope? Oh, your handkerchief, so it is. [*Searching next* PRISONER.] You here, what's this? A bit of wax end, you forgot to leave in the bag shop? Well, don't forget the next time. What's this? [MAN *takes out two inches of rope.*] What's this for? You were roping mail bags today, and after all they don't rope themselves. Ah, you forgot to leave it behind? Well, go easy, save as much as that each time and in five years' time you'd have enough to make a rope ladder. Oh, you're only doing six months? Well maybe you want to save the taxpayers a few quid and hang yourself. Sorrow the loss if you did, but they'd want to know where you got the rope from. [PRISONERS *laugh as they are expected to do.*] Come on, next man. [*He hurries along now.*] Come along now, no mailbags, scissors, needles, knives, razor blades, guns, hatchets or empty porter bottles. No? [*To the last* PRISONER.] Well, will you buy a ticket to the Police Ball?

PRISONERS *laugh dutifully.*

WARDER REGAN [*voice from prison wing*]. All done, sir?

PRISONER A. Don't forget, Neighbour.

WARDER DONELLY. Right, sir, on to you, sir. [*Gate swings open.*] Right, lead on, B.1.

NEIGHBOUR. Anyway, his grave's dug and the hangman's on his way.

PRISONER A. That doesn't mean a thing, they always dig the grave, just to put the wind up them—

WARDER DONELLY. Silence!

The prisoners march, the gate clangs behind them; the tramp of their feet is heard as they mark time inside.

WARDER REGAN [*voice from the prison wing*]. Right, B. Wing, bang out your doors. B.1, get in off your steps and bang out your doors, into your cells and bang out your doors. Get locked up. BANG THEM DOORS! GET INSIDE AND BANG OUT THEM DOORS!

The last door bangs lonely on its own and then there is silence.

VOICE FROM BELOW [*singing*].

> The wind was rising,
> And the day declining
> As I lay pining in my prison cell
> And that old triangle
> Went jingle jangle

The triangle is beaten, the gate of the prison wing opens and the CHIEF *and* WARDER DONELLY *come down the steps and approach the grave.*

> Along the banks of the Royal Canal.

CHIEF [*resplendent in silver braid*]. Who's that singing?

WARDER DONELLY. I think it's one of the prisoners in the chokey, sir.

CHIEF. Where?

WARDER DONELLY. In the punishment cells, sir.

CHIEF. That's more like it. Well, tell him to cut it out.

SONG.

> In the female prison
> There are seventy women . . .

WARDER DONELLY [*goes down to the area and leans and shouts*]. Hey, you down there, cut it out, or I'll give you jingle jangle.

The song stops. WARDER DONELLY *walks back.*

CHIEF. Is the quare fellow finished his tea?

WARDER DONELLY. He is. He is just ready to come out for exercise, now. The wings are all clear. They're locked up having their tea. He'll be along any minute.

CHIEF. He's coming out here?

WARDER DONELLY. Yes, sir.

CHIEF [*exasperated*]. Do you want him to see his grave, bloody well half dug? Run in quick and tell those bloody idiots to take him out the side door, and exercise him over the far side of the stokehold, and tell them to keep him well into the wall where he'll be out of sight of the cell windows. Hurry and don't let him hear you. Let on it's something about another duty. Warders! You'd get better in Woolworths.

He goes to the area and shouts down.

Hey, you down there. You in the cell under the steps. You do be singing there to keep yourself company? You needn't be afraid, it's only the Chief. How long you doing down there? Seven days No. 1 and twenty-one days No. 2. God bless us and love us, you must have done something desperate. I may be able to do something for you, though God knows you needn't count on it, I don't own the place. You what? With who? Ah sure, I often have a bit of a tiff with the same man myself. We'll see what we can do for you. It's a long time to be stuck down there, no matter who you had the tiff with.

Enter WARDER DONELLY.

CHIEF. Well?

WARDER DONELLY. It's all right, they've brought him out the other way.

They look out beyond the stage.

CHIEF. Looks as if they're arguing the toss about something.

WARDER DONELLY. Football.

CHIEF. Begod, look at them stopping while the quare fellow hammers his point home.

WARDER DONELLY. I was down in the condemned cell while he was getting his tea. I asked him if it was all right. He said it was, and "Aren't the evenings getting a grand stretch?" he says.

CHIEF. Look at him now, putting his nose to the air.

WARDER DONELLY. He's a grand evening for his last.

CHIEF. I took the name of the fellow giving the concert in the punishment cells. In the morning when we get this over, see he's shifted to Hell's gates over the far side. He can serenade the stokehold wall for a change if he's light enough to make out his music.

WARDER DONELLY *copies the name and number.*

CHIEF. I have to attend to every mortal thing in this place. None of youse seem to want to do a hand's turn, bar draw your money—you're quick enough at that. Well, come on, let's get down to business.

WARDER DONELLY *goes and uncovers the grave.*

CHIEF [*looking off*]. Just a minute. It's all right. They've taken him round the back of the stokehold. [*Looking at the grave.*] Not so bad, another couple of feet out of the bottom and we're elected. Regan should be down with the working party any minute, as soon as the quare fellow's finished his exercise.

WARDER DONELLY. There, he's away in now, sir. See him looking at the sky?

CHIEF. You'd think he was trying to kiss it good-bye. Well, that's the last he'll see of it.

WARDER DONELLY. No chance of a reprieve, sir?

CHIEF. Not a chance. Healey never even mentioned fixing up a line with the Post Office. If there'd been any chance of developments he'd have asked us to put a man on all night. All he said was "The Governor will get the last word before the night's out." That means only one thing. Go ahead.

WARDERS REGAN *and* CRIMMIN *come out with* PRISONERS A. B. C. *and* D.

WARDER REGAN. Working party all correct, sir. Come on, get those boards off. Bottom out a couple more feet and leave the clay at the top, nice and neat.

CHIEF. Oh, Mr. Regan.

WARDER REGAN. Take over, Mr. Crimmin.

CHIEF. Mr. Regan. All I was going to say was—why don't

you take yourself a bit of a rest while these fellows are at work on the grave. It's a long old pull till eight tomorrow morning.

WARDER REGAN. Thank you, sir.

CHIEF. Don't mention it. I'll see you before you go down to the cell. Get yourself a bit of a smoke, in the hospital. Don't forget now.

He *and* WARDER DONELLY *go back in.*

WARDER REGAN. Mr. Crimmin. The Chief, a decent man, he's after giving us his kind permission to go into hospital and have a sit down and a smoke for ourselves when these fellows have the work started. He knew we'd go in anyway, so he saw the chance of being floochalach, at no expense to the management. Here [*Takes out a packet of cigarettes, and takes some from it.*], here's a few fags for the lads.

CRIMMIN. I'll give them some of mine too.

WARDER REGAN. Don't do anything of the sort. One each is enough, you can slip them a couple when they're going to be locked up, if you like, but if these fellows had two fags each, they'd not work at all but spend the time out here blowing smoke rings in the evening air like lords. I'll slip in now, you come in after me. Tell them not to have them in their mouths if the Chief or the Governor comes out.

He goes up the steps to the hospital.

CRIMMIN [*calls* PRISONER C.) Hey!

PRISONER C. [*comes to him*]. Seadh a Thomais?

CRIMMIN [*gives him cigarettes and matches*]. Seo, cupla toitin[1] Taim fhein is an scew eile ag dul isteach chuig an cispeadeal, noimeat. Roinn amach na toitini siud, is

[1] For translation of the Gaelic dialogue see page 87

glacfhaidh sibh gal. Mathagann an Governor no'n Chief no an Principal, na biodh in bhur moeil agaibh iad. A' tuigeann tu?

PRISONER C. Tuigim, a Thomais, go raibh maith agat.

CRIMMIN. [*officially*]. Right, now get back to your work.

PRISONER C. Yes, sir.

CRIMMIN *goes up the hospital steps.*

PRISONER C. He gave me some cigarettes.

PRISONER D. *has gone straight to the grave,* PRISONER B. *is near it.*

PRISONER A. May I never dig a grave for less! You two get on and do a bit of digging while we have a quiet burn, then we'll take over.

PRISONER C. He said to watch out for the chief and them.

PRISONER B. Pass down a light to your man. He says he'd enjoy it better down there, where he can't be seen! Decent of him and Regan wasn't it?

PRISONER A. They'd have you dead from decency. That same Regan was like a savage in the bag shop today, you couldn't get a word to the fellow next to you.

PRISONER C. I never saw him like that before.

PRISONER B. He's always the same at a time like this, hanging seems to get on his nerves.

PRISONER A. Why should he worry, he won't feel it.

PRISONER B. He's on the last watch. Twelve till eight.

PRISONER A. Till death do us part.

PRISONER C. The quare fellow asked for him, didn't he?

PRISONER A. They all do.

PRISONER C. He asked to have Mr. Crimmin too.

PRISONER A. It'll break that young screw up, and him only a wet day in the place.

PRISONER B. Funny the way they all ask for Regan. Perhaps they think he'll bring them good luck, him being good living.

PRISONER A. Good living! Whoever heard of a good living screw? Did you never hear of the screw, married the prostitute?

PRISONER B. No, what happened to him?

PRISONER A. He dragged her down to his own level.

PRISONER B. He told me once that if I kept off the beer I need never come back here. I asked him what about himself, and he told me he was terrible hardened to it and would I pray for him.

PRISONER C. When I was over in the Juveniles he used to talk like that to us. He said that the Blessed Virgin knew us better than the police or the judges—or ourselves even. We might think we were terrible sinners but she knew we were good boys only a bit wild . . .

PRISONER A. Bloody mad he is.

PRISONER C. And that we were doing penance here for the men who took us up, especially the judges, they being mostly rich old men with great opportunity for vice.

> PRISONER D. *appears from the grave.*

PRISONER A. The dead arose and appeared to many.

> PRISONER A. *goes and rearranges the work which* PRISONER D. *has upset.*

PRISONER B. What's brought you out of your fox hole?

PRISONER D. I thought it more discreet to remain in concealment while I smoked but I could not stop down there listening to talk like that, as a ratepayer, I couldn't stand for it, especially those libellous remarks about the judiciary.

He looks accusingly at the boy.

PRISONER C. I was only repeating what Mr. Regan said, sir.

PRISONER D. He could be taken up for it. According to that man, there should be no such thing as law and order. We could all be murdered in our beds, the innocent prey of every ruffian that took it into his head to appropriate our goods, our lives even. Property must have security! What do you think society would come to without police and judges and suitable punishments? Chaos! In my opinion hanging's too good for 'em.

PRISONER C. Oh, Mr. Regan doesn't believe in capital punishment, sir.

PRISONER D. My God, the man's an atheist! He should be dismissed from the public service. I shall take it up with the Minister when I get out of here. I went to school with his cousin.

PRISONER A. Who the hell does he think he is, a bloody high court judge?

PRISONER D. Chaos!

PRISONER B. He's in for embezzlement, there were two suicides and a bye-election over him.

PRISONER D. There are still a few of us who care about the state of the country, you know. My family's national tradition goes back to the Land War. Grandfather did four weeks for incitement to mutiny—and we've never looked back since. One of my young nephews, as a matter of fact, has just gone over to Sandhurst.

PRISONER B. Isn't that where you done your four years?

PRISONER A. No, that was Parkhurst.

PRISONER C. [*to others*]. A college educated man in here, funny, isn't it?

PRISONER D. I shall certainly bring all my influence to bear to settle this Regan fellow.

PRISONER C. You must be a very important man, sir.

PRISONER D. I am one of the Cashel Carrolls, my boy, related on my mother's side to the Killens of Killcock.

PRISONER B. Used to wash for our family.

PRISONER C. Go bhfoiridh Dia 'rainn.

PRISONER D. Irish speaking?

PRISONER C. Yes, sir.

PRISONER D. Then it might interest you to know that I took my gold medal in Irish.

PRISONER C. Does that mean he speaks Irish?

PRISONER D. Of course.

PRISONER C. Oh sir. Ta Gaeilge go leor agamsa. O'n gcliabhain amach, sir.

PRISONER B. That's fixed you.

PRISONER D. Quite. Tuigim tu.

PRISONER B. The young lad's from Kerry, from an island where they don't speak much else.

PRISONER D. Kerry? Well of course you speak with a different dialect to the one I was taught.

PRISONER B. The young screw Crimmin's from the same place. He sneaks up to the landing sometimes when the other screws aren't watching and there they are for hours talking through the spy hole, all in Irish.

PRISONER D. Most irregular.

PRISONER B. There's not much harm in it.

PRISONER D. How can there be proper discipline between warder and prisoner with that kind of familiarity?

PRISONER C. He does only be giving me the news from home and who's gone to America or England; he's not long up here and neither am I . . . the two of us do each be as lonely as the other.

PRISONER B. The lad here sings an old song betimes. It's very nice. It makes the night less lonely, each man alone and sad maybe in the old cell. The quare fellow heard him singing and after he was sentenced to death he sent over word he'd be listening every night around midnight for him.

PRISONER A. You'd better make a bit effort tonight, kid, for his last concert.

PRISONER C. Ah, God help him! Sure, you'd pity him all the same. It must be awful to die at the end of a swinging rope and a black hood over his poor face.

PRISONER A. Begod, he's not being topped for nothing—to cut his own brother up and butcher him like a pig.

PRISONER D. I must heartily agree with you sir, a barbarian if ever there was one.

PRISONER C. Maybe he did those things, but God help him this minute and he knowing this night his last on earth. Waiting over there he is, to be shaken out of his sleep and rushed to the rope.

PRISONER A. What sleep will he take? They won't have to set the alarm clock for a quarter to eight, you can bet your life on that.

PRISONER C. May he find peace on the other side.

PRISONER A. Or his brother waiting to have a word with him about being quartered in such an unmannerly fashion.

PRISONER C. None of us can know for certain.

PRISONER D. It was proved in a court of law that this man had experience as a pork butcher and put his expert knowledge to use by killing his brother with an axe and dismembering the body, the better to dispose of it.

PRISONER C. Go bfoiridh. Dia rainn.

PRISONER A. I wouldn't put much to the court of law part of it, but I heard about it myself from a fellow in from his part of the country. He said he had the brother strung up in an outhouse like a pig.

PRISONER D. Actually he was bleeding him into a farm-house vessel according to the evidence. He should be hung three or four times over.

PRISONER A. Seeing your uncle was at school with the President's granny, perhaps he could fix it up for you.

PRISONER C. I don't believe he is a bad man. When I was on remand he used to walk around with me at exercise every day and he was sad when I told him about my brother, who died in the Yank's army, and my father, who was buried alive at the demolition of Manchester . . . He was great company for me who knew no one, only jackeens would be making game of me, and I'm sorry for him.

PRISONER A. Sure, it's a terrible pity about you and him. Maybe the jackeens should spread out the red carpet for you and every other bog barbarian that comes into the place.

He moves away irritably.

Let's get a bit more off this bloody hole.

PRISONER B. Nick. Nick.

WARDER REGAN [*entering with* CRIMMIN]. I've been watching you for the last ten minutes and damn the thing you've done except yap, yap, yap the whole time. The

E

Chief or the Governor or any of them could have been watching you. They'd have thought it was a bloody mothers' meeting. What with you and my other bald mahogany gas pipe here.

PRISONER D. We were merely exchanging a few comments, sir.

WARDER REGAN. That's a lie and it's not worth a lie.

PRISONER A. All right! So we were caught talking at labour. I didn't ask to be an undertaker's assistant. Go on, bang me inside and case me in the morning! Let the Governor give me three days of No. 1.

WARDER REGAN. Much that'd worry you.

PRISONER A. You're dead right.

WARDER REGAN. Don't be such a bloody big baby. We all know you're a hard case. Where did you do your lagging? On the bog?

PRISONER A. I did not. Two laggings I done! At Parkhurst and on the Moor.

WARDER REGAN. There's the national inferiority complex for you. Our own Irish cat-o'-nine-tails and the batons of the warders loaded with lead from Carrick mines aren't good enough for him. He has to go Dartmooring and Parkhursting it. It's a wonder you didn't go further while you were at it, to Sing Sing or Devil's Island.

PRISONER A. [stung]. I'm not here to be made a mock of, whether I done a lagging in England or not.

WARDER REGAN. Who said a word about it, only your-self—doing the returned Yank in front of these other fellows? Look, the quare fellow's got to be buried in the morning, whether we like it or not, so cut the mullarkey and get back to work.

PRISONER A. I don't let anyone make game of me!

WARDER REGAN. Well, what are you going to do about it? Complain to Holy Healey's department? He's a fine bloody imposter, isn't he? Like an old I.R.A. man with a good agency in the Sweep now. Recommend me to the respectable people! Drop it for Christ's sake, man. It's a bad night for all of us. Fine job, isn't it, for a young fellow like him, fresh from his mother's apron strings. You haven't forgotten what it's like to come from a decent home, have you, with the family rosary said every night?

PRISONER A. I haven't any time for that kind of gab. I never saw religion do anything but back up the screws. I was in Walton last Christmas Eve, when the clergyman came to visit a young lad that had been given eighteen strokes of the cat that morning. When the kid stopped moaning long enough to hear what he had to say, he was told to think on the Lord's sufferings, then the cell door closed with a bang, leaving a smell of booze that would have tripped you up.

He takes a look at the quare fellow's side of the stage and, muttering to himself, goes back to work.

WARDER REGAN. You should pray for a man hardened in drink. Get back to it, all of you, and get that work a bit more advanced. Myself and Crimmin here have a long night ahead of us; we don't want to be finishing off your jobs for you.

They get into the grave.

PRISONER A. I never seen a screw like that before.

PRISONER B. Neither did anyone else.

They work.

CRIMMIN. What time is it, sir?

WARDER REGAN. Ten to seven.

CRIMMIN. Is himself here yet?

WARDER REGAN. Yes, he came by last night's boat. He's nervous of the 'plane, says it isn't natural. He'll be about soon. He's been having a sleep after the trip. We'll have to wait till he's measured the quare fellow for the drop, then we can go off till twelve.

CRIMMIN. Good.

WARDER REGAN. And for Christ's sake try to look a bit more cheerful when you come back on.

CRIMMIN. I've never seen anyone die, Mr. Regan.

WARDER REGAN. Of course, I'm a callous savage that's used to it.

CRIMMIN. I didn't mean that.

WARDER REGAN. I don't like it now any more than I did the first time.

CRIMMIN. No sir.

WARDER REGAN. It was a little Protestant lad, the first time; he asked if he could be walked backwards into the hanghouse so as he wouldn't see the rope.

CRIMMIN. God forgive them.

WARDER REGAN. May He forgive us all. The young clergy-man that was on asked if the prison chaplain could accompany him; it was his first hanging too. I went to the Canon to ask him, a fine big man he was. "Regan," he says, "I thought I was going to escape it this time, but you never escape. I don't suppose neither of us ever will. Ah well," he says, "maybe being hung twenty times will get me out of purgatory a minute or two sooner."

CRIMMIN. Amen, a Thighearna Dhia.

WARDER REGAN. The young clergyman was great; he read a bit of the Bible to the little Protestant lad while they waited and he came in with him, holding his hand and telling him, in their way, to lean on God's mercy that was stronger than the power of men. I walked beside them and guided the boy on to the trap and under the beam. The rope was put round him and the washer under his ear and the hood pulled over his face. And still the young clergyman called out to him, in a grand steady voice, in through the hood: "I declare to you, my living Christ this night . . ." and he stroked his head till he went down. Then he fainted; the Canon and myself had to carry him out to the Governor's office.

A pause. We are aware of the men working at the grave.

WARDER REGAN. The quare fellow asked for you especially, Crimmin; he wanted you because you're a young lad, not yet practised in badness. You'll be a consolation to him in the morning when he's surrounded by a crowd of bigger bloody ruffians than himself, if the truth were but told. He's depending on you, and you're going to do your best for him.

CRIMMIN. Yes, Mr. Regan.

REGAN *walks to the grave.*

WARDER REGAN. How's it going?

PRISONER A. Just about done, sir.

WARDER REGAN. All right, you can leave it.

They get up.

WARDER REGAN. Leave your shovels; you'll be wanting them in the morning. Go and tell the warder they've finished, Mr. Crimmin. I'll turn them over.

He searches the PRISONERS, *finds a cigarette end on* A. *and sniffs it.*

Coffin nail. Most appropriate. [*He goes towards exit and calls.*] You needn't bother searching them, sir. I've turned them over.

PRISONER A. [*aside*]. He's as mad as a coot.

PRISONER C. But charitable.

WARDER REGAN. Right, lead on there!

PRISONER D. This is no place for charity, on the taxpayers' money.

PRISONER A. Take it up with your uncle when you get back into your stockbroker's trousers.

WARDER REGAN. Silence. Right, sir, working party off.

As the PRISONERS *march off, the* HANGMAN *comes slowly down the steps.*

CRIMMIN. Is this . . .

WARDER REGAN. Himself.

HANGMAN. It's Mr. Regan, isn't it? Well, as the girl said to the soldier "Here we are again."

WARDER REGAN. Nice evening. I hope you had a good crossing.

HANGMAN. Not bad. It's nice to get over to old Ireland you know, a nice bit of steak and a couple of pints as soon as you get off the boat. Well, you'll be wanting to knock off, won't you? I'll just pop down and have a look, then you can knock off.

WARDER REGAN. We were just waiting for you.

HANGMAN. This young man coming with us in the morning?

CRIMMIN. Yes, sir.

HANGMAN. Lend us your cap a minute, lad.

CRIMMIN. I don't think it would fit you, sir.

HANGMAN. We don't have to be so particular. Mr. Regan's will do. It ought to fit me by this time, and he won't catch cold the time I'll be away.

He goes out.

CRIMMIN. What does he want the cap for?

WARDER REGAN. He gets the quare fellow's weight from the doctor so as he'll know what drop to give him, but he likes to have a look at him as well, to see what build he is, how thick his neck is, and so on. He says he can judge better with the eye. If he gave him too much one way he'd strangle him instead of breaking his neck, and too much the other way he'd pull the head clean off his shoulders.

CRIMMIN. Go bhfoiridh Dia 'rainn.

WARDER REGAN. You should have lent him your cap. When he lifts the corner of the spy-hole all the quare fellow can see is the peak of a warder's cap. It could be you or me or anyone looking at him. Himself has no more to do with it than you or I or the people that pay us, and that's every man or woman that pays taxes or votes in elections. If they don't like it, they needn't have it.

The HANGMAN *comes back.*

HANGMAN. Well set up lad. Twelve stone, fine pair of shoulders on him. Well, I expect you'll give us a call this evening over at the hospital. I'm in my usual apartments. This young man is very welcome, too, if he wants to join the company.

WARDER REGAN. Right, sir.

HANGMAN. See you later.

He goes out.

WARDER REGAN. Right, Crimmin. Twelve o'clock and look lively. The quare fellow's got enough on his plate without putting him in the blue jigs altogether. As the old Home Office memorandum says "An air of cheerful decorum is indicated, as a readiness to play such games as draughts, ludo, or snakes and ladders; a readiness to enter into conversations on sporting topics will also be appreciated."

CRIMMIN. Yes, sir.

WARDER REGAN. [as they go]. And, Crimmin, . . .

CRIMMIN. Yes, sir?

WARDER REGAN. Take off your watch.

They go out.

NEIGHBOUR [from his cell]. Hey, Dunlavin. Don't forget that Sunday bacon. The bet stands. They're after being at the grave. I just heard them. Dunlavin, do you hear me?

PRISONER A. Get down on your bed, you old Anti-Christ. You sound like something in a week-end pass out of Hell.

ENGLISH PRISONER. Hey, you bloke that's going out in the morning. Don't forget to see my chiner and get him to bail me out.

NEIGHBOUR. Get a bucket and bail yourself out.

SONG.   The day was dying and the wind was sighing,
                As I lay crying in my prison cell,
                And the old triangle
                Went jingle jangle
                Along the banks of the Royal Canal.

The curtain falls

ACT III

Scene One

Later the same night. Cell windows lit. A blue lamp in the courtyard. A faint tapping is heard intermittently.

As the curtain rises, two WARDERS *are seen. One is* DONELLY, *the other a fellow new to the job.*

WARDER 1. Watch the match.

WARDER 2. Sorry.

WARDER 1. We're all right for a couple of minutes, the Chief'll have plenty to worry him tonight; he's not likely to be prowling about.

WARDER 2. Hell of a job, night patrol, at any time.

WARDER 1. We're supposed to pass each cell every half-hour tonight, but what's the use? Listen to 'em.

The tapping can be distinctly heard.

WARDER 2. Yap, yap, yap. It's a wonder the bloody old hot-water pipes aren't worn through.

Tapping.

WARDER 1. Damn it all, they've been yapping in association since seven o'clock.

Tapping.

WARDER 2. Will I go round the landings and see who it is?

WARDER 1. See who it is? Listen!

WARDER 2. Do you think I should go?

WARDER 1. Stay where you are and get yourself a bit of a burn. Devil a bit of use it'd be anyway. As soon as you lifted the first spy-hole, the next fellow would have heard you and passed it on to the whole landing. Mind the cigarette, keep it covered. Have you ever been in one of these before?

WARDER 2. No.

WARDER 1. They'll be at it from six o'clock tomorrow morning, and when it comes a quarter to eight it'll be like a running commentary in the Grand National.

Tapping.

WARDER 1 [*quietly*]. Shut your bloody row! And then the screeches and roars of them when his time comes. They say it's the last thing the fellow hears.

Tapping dies down.

WARDER 2. Talk about something else.

Tapping.

WARDER 1. They're quietening down a bit. You'd think they'd be in the humour for a read or a sleep, wouldn't you?

WARDER 2. It's a hell of a job.

WARDER 1. We're in it for the three P's, boy, pay, promotion and pension, that's all that should bother civil servants like us.

WARDER 2. You're quite right.

WARDER 1. And without doing the sergeant major on you, I'm senior man of us two, isn't that right, now?

WARDER 2. I know what you mean.

WARDER 1. Well, neither bragging nor boasting—God gives

us the brains and no credit to ourselves—I think I might speak to you as a senior man, if you didn't mind.

WARDER 2. Not at all. Any tip you could give me I'd be only too grateful for it. Sure it'd only be a thick wouldn't improve his knowledge when an older man would be willing to tell him something that would be of benefit to him in his career.

WARDER 1. Well now, would I be right in saying that you've no landing of your own?

WARDER 2. Quite right, quite right. I'm only on here, there or any old where when you or any other senior man is wanting me.

WARDER 1. Well, facts is facts and must be faced. We must all creep before we can walk, as the man said; but I may as well tell you straight, what I told the Principal about you.

WARDER 2. Tell me face to face. If it's fault you found in me I'd as lief hear it from me friend as from me enemy.

WARDER 1. It was no fault I found in you. If I couldn't do a man a good turn—I'd be sorry to do him a bad one.

WARDER 2. Ah, sure I know that.

WARDER 1. What I said to the Principal about you was: that you could easily handle a landing of your own. If it happened that one was left vacant. And I don't think I'm giving official information away, when I say that such a vacancy may occur in the near future. Before the month is out. Have you me?

WARDER 2. I have you, and I'm more than grateful to you. But sure I'd expect no less from you. You're all nature.

WARDER 1. It might happen that our Principal was going to the Bog on promotion, and it might happen that a certain senior officer would be promoted in his place.

WARDER 2. Ah, no.

WARDER 1. But ah, yes.

WARDER 2. But there's no one in the prison but'd be delighted to serve under you. You've such a way with you. Even with the prisoners.

WARDER 1. Well, I hope I can do my best by me fellow men, and that's the most any can hope to do, barring a double-dyed bloody hypocrite like a certain party we needn't mention. Well, him and me have equal service and it's only the one of us can be made Principal, and I'm damn sure they're not going to appoint a half-lunatic that goes round asking murderers to pray for him.

WARDER 2. Certainly they're not, unless they're bloody-well half-mad themselves.

WARDER 1. And I think they know him as well as we do.

WARDER 2. Except the Canon, poor man; he has him well recommended.

WARDER 1. You can leave out the "poor man" part of it. God forgive me and I renounce the sin of it, the Lord says "touch not my anointed", but the Canon is a bloody sight worse than himself, if you knew only the half of it.

WARDER 2. Go to God.

WARDER 1. Right, I'll tell you now. He was silenced for something before he came here and this is the *only* job he can get. Something terrible he did, though God forgive us, maybe it's not right to talk of it.

WARDER 2. You might sing it.

WARDER 1. I hear it was the way that he made the house-keeper take a girl into the house, the priest's house, to have a baby, an illegitimate!

WARDER 2. And could a man like that be fit to be a priest!

WARDER 1. He'd hardly be fit to be a prison chaplain, even. Here's the Chief or one of them coming. Get inside quick and let on you're looking for them fellows talking on the hot-water pipes, and not a word about what I said. That's between ourselves.

WARDER 2. Ah sure I know that's under foot. Thanks anyway.

WARDER 1. You're more than welcome. Don't be surprised if you get your landing sooner than you expected. Thirty cells all to yourself before you're fifty.

WARDER 2. I'll have the sister's children pray for you.

Enter CHIEF WARDER.

WARDER 1. All correct, sir.

CHIEF. What the hell do you mean, "All correct, sir"? I've been watching you this half-hour yapping away to that other fellow.

WARDER 1. There were men communicating on the hot-water pipes, sir, and I told him ten times if I told him once to go inside the landing and see who it was; it's my opinion, sir, the man is a bit thick.

CHIEF. It's your opinion. Well, you're that thick yourself you ought to be a fair judge. And who the bloody hell are you to tell anyone to do anything? You're on night patrol the same as what he is.

WARDER 1. I thought, sir, on account of the night that's in it.

CHIEF. Why, is it Christmas? Listen here, that there is an execution in the morning is nothing to do with you. It's not your job to care, and a good job too, or you'd probably trip over the rope and fall through the bloody trap. What business have you out here, anyway?

WARDER 1. I thought I had to patrol by the grave, sir.

CHIEF. Afraid somebody might pinch it? True enough, this place is that full of thieves, you can leave nothing out of your hand. Get inside and resume your patrol. If you weren't one of the old hands I'd report you to the Governor. Get along with you and we'll forget about it.

WARDER 1. Very good, sir, and thank you, sir.

> *Tapping.*

CHIEF. And stop that tapping on the pipes.

WARDER 1. I will, sir, and thanks again, sir.

> FIRST WARDER *salutes, goes up the steps to the prison gates, which open. The* GOVERNOR *comes in in evening dress. The* FIRST WARDER *comes sharply to attention, salutes and goes off. The* GOVERNOR *continues down the steps and over to the* CHIEF WARDER.

CHIEF. All correct, sir.

GOVERNOR. Good. We had final word about the reprieve this afternoon. But you know how these things are, Chief, hoping for last-minute developments. I must say I should have been more than surprised had the Minister made a recommendation. I'll go down and see him before the Canon comes in. It makes them more settled for confession when they know there is absolutely no hope. How is he?

CHIEF. Very well, sir. Sitting by the fire and chatting to the warders. He says he might go to bed after he sees the priest.

GOVERNOR. You'll see that there's a good breakfast for himself and the two assistants?

CHIEF. Oh, yes, sir, he's very particular about having two rashers and eggs. Last time they were here, some hungry pig ate half his breakfast and he kicked up murder.

GOVERNOR. See it doesn't happen this time.

CHIEF. No indeed. There's a fellow under sentence of death next week in the Crumlin; we don't want him going up to Belfast and saying we starved him.

GOVERNOR. Have they come back from town yet?

CHIEF [*looks at his watch*]. It's after closing time. I don't expect they'll be long now. I put Clancy on the side gate to let them in. After he took the quare fellow's measurements he went over to the place he drinks in. Some pub at the top of Grafton Street. I believe he's the life of the bar there, sir; the customers think he's an English traveller. The publican knows who he is, but then they're both in the pub business, and sure that's as tight a trade as hanging.

GOVERNOR. I suppose his work here makes him philosophical, and they say that drink is the comfort of the philosophers.

CHIEF. I wouldn't doubt but you'd be right there, sir. But he told me himself he only takes a drink when he's on a job. The rest of the time he's serving behind his own bar.

GOVERNOR. Is Jenkinson with him?

CHIEF. Yes, sir. He likes to have him with him, in case he gets a bit jarred. Once he went straight from the boat to the pubs and spent the day in them, and when he got here wasn't he after leaving the black box with his rope and his washers and his other little odds and ends behind him in a pub and forgot which one it was he left them in.

GOVERNOR. Really.

CHIEF. You could sing it. You were in Limerick at the time, sir, but here we were, in a desperate state. An execution coming off in the morning and we without the black box that had all his tools in it. The Governor we had then, he promised a novena to St. Anthony and two insertions in the *Messenger* if they were found in time. And sure enough after squad cars were all over in the city, the box was got in a pub down the North Wall, the first one he went into. It shows you the power of prayer, sir.

GOVERNOR. Yes, I see what you mean.

CHIEF. So now he always brings Jenkinson with him. You see, Jenkinson takes nothing, being very good living. A street preacher he is, for the Methodists or something. Himself prefers T.T.s. He had an Irishman from Clare helping one time, but he sacked him over the drink. In this Circus, he said, there's only one allowed to drink and that's the Ringmaster.

GOVERNOR. We advertised for a native hangman during the Economic War. Must be fluent Irish speaker. Cailioctai de reir Meamram V. a seacht. There were no suitable applicants.

CHIEF. By the way, sir, I must tell you that the warders on night patrol were out here conversing, instead of going round the landings.

GOVERNOR. Remind me to make a note of it tomorrow.

CHIEF. I will, sir, and I think I ought to tell you that I heard the principal warder make a joke about the execution.

GOVERNOR. Good God, this sort of thing is getting out of hand. I was at my School Union this evening. I had to leave in sheer embarrassment; supposedly witty remarks made to me at my own table. My eldest son was furious with me for going at all. He was at a table with a crowd from the University. They were even worse. One young pup went so far as to ask him if he thought I would oblige with a rendering of "The night before Larry was stretched". I shall certainly tell the Principal that there's at least one place in this city where an execution is taken very seriously indeed. Good night to you.

CHIEF. Good night, sir.

> *Tapping. The* CHIEF WARDER *walks up and down.* REGAN *enters.*

Ah, Mr. Regan, the other man coming along?

WARDER REGAN. He'll be along in a minute.

CHIEF. I don't know what we'd do without you, Regan, on these jobs. Is there anything the Governor or I could do to make things easier?

WARDER REGAN. You could say a decade of the rosary.

CHIEF. I could hardly ask the Governor to do that.

WARDER REGAN. His prayers would be as good as anyone else's.

CHIEF. Is there anything on the practical side we could send down?

WARDER REGAN. A bottle of malt.

CHIEF. Do you think he'd drink it?

WARDER REGAN. No, but I would.

CHIEF. Regan, I'm surprised at you.

WARDER REGAN. I was reared among people that drank at a death or prayed. Some did both. You think the law makes this man's death someway different, not like any-one else's. Your own, for instance.

CHIEF. I wasn't found guilty of murder.

WARDER REGAN. No, nor no one is going to jump on you in the morning and throttle the life out of you, but it's not him I'm thinking of. It's myself. And you're not going to give me that stuff about just shoving over the lever and

F

bob's your uncle. You forget the times the fellow gets caught and has to be kicked off the edge of the trap hole. You never heard of the warders down below swinging on his legs the better to break his neck, or jumping on his back when the drop was too short.

CHIEF. Mr. Regan, I'm surprised at you.

WARDER REGAN. That's the second time tonight.

Tapping. Enter CRIMMIN.

CRIMMIN. All correct, sir.

CHIEF. Regan, I hope you'll forget those things you mentioned just now. If talk the like of that got outside the prison . . .

WARDER REGAN [*almost shouts*]. I think the whole show should be put on in Croke Park; after all, it's at the public expense and they let it go on. They should have something more for their money than a bit of paper stuck up on the gate.

CHIEF. Good night, Regan. If I didn't know you, I'd report what you said to the Governor.

WARDER REGAN. You will anyway.

CHIEF. Good night, Regan.

WARDER REGAN [*to* CRIMMIN]. Crimmin, there you are. I'm going into the hospital to fix up some supper for us. An empty sack won't stand, as the man said, nor a full one won't bend.

He goes. CRIMMIN *strolls. Traffic is heard in the distance. drowning the tapping. A drunken crowd are heard singing.* DONELLY *and the* NEW WARDER *appear in the darkness.*

WARDER 1. Is that young Mr. Crimmin?

CRIMMIN. Yes, it's me.

WARDER 1. You've a desperate job for a young warder this night. But I'll tell you one thing, you've a great man with you. Myself and this other man here are only after being talking about him.

WARDER 2. That's right, so we were. A grand man and very good living.

WARDER 1. There's someone coming. Too fine a night to be indoors. Good night, Mr. Crimmin.

CRIMMIN. Good night, sir.

WARDER 1 [*as they go off*]. Come on, let's get a sup of tea.

> CRIMMIN *waits. Tapping heard.* WARDER REGAN *re-enters.*

WARDER REGAN. Supper's fixed. It's a fine clear night. Do you hear the buses? Fellows leaving their mot's home, after the pictures or coming from dances, and a few old fellows well jarred but half sober for fear of what herself will say when they get in the door. Only a hundred yards up there on the bridge, and it might as well be a hundred miles away. Here they are back from the pub.

> *Voices are heard in the dark approaching. Enter* HANG-MAN *and* JENKINSON.

HANGMAN [*sings*].
"She was lovely and fair like the rose of the summer,
Though 'twas not her beauty alone that won me,
Oh, no, 'twas the truth in her eyes ever shining,
That made me love Mary the Rose of Tralee."
Don't see any signs of Regan.

JENKINSON. He's probably had to go on duty. You've left it too late.

HANGMAN. Well, if the mountain won't come to M'ammed then the M'ammed must go to the mountain.

WARDER REGAN [*from the darkness*]. As the girl said to the soldier.

HANGMAN. As the girl said to the soldier. Oh, it's you, Regan. Will you have a drink?

WARDER REGAN. I'm afraid we've got to be off now.

HANGMAN. Never mind off now. Have one with me. It's a pleasure to see you again. We meet all too seldom. You have one with me. Adam, give him a bottle of stout.

>   *He sings again.*

>   "Oh, no, 'twas the truth in her eyes ever shining,
>   That made me love Mary the Rose of Tralee."

Not bad for an old 'un. Lovely song, in't it? Very religious though. "The Poor Christian Fountain." I'm very fond of the old Irish songs; we get a lot of Irish in our place on a Saturday night, you know.

WARDER REGAN. Is it what they call a sporting pub?

HANGMAN. That's just what it is, and an old sport behind the bar counter an' all. All the Irish come in, don't they, Adam?

JENKINSON [*gloomily*]. Reckon they do. Perhaps because no one else would go in it.

HANGMAN. What do you mean? It's best beer in the district. Not that you could tell the difference.

WARDER REGAN. Good health.

HANGMAN. May we never do worse. [*To* JENKINSON.] You're in a right cut, aren't you, making out there's nobody but Irish coming into my pub? I've never wanted for friends. Do you know why? Because I'd go a 'undred mile to do a man a good turn. I've always tried to do my duty.

JENKINSON. And so have I.

HANGMAN. Do you remember the time I got out from a sickbed to 'ang a soldier at Strangeways, when I thought you and Christmas 'adn't had enough experience?

JENKINSON. Aye, that's right enough.

HANGMAN. I'm not going to quarrel with you. Here, go
and fetch your concertina and sing 'em that hymn you
composed.

JENKINSON *hesitates.*

HANGMAN. Go on. It's a grand tune, a real credit to you.
Go on, lad.

JENKINSON. Well, only for the hymn, mind.

He goes off to fetch it.

WARDER REGAN. Sure, that's right.

HANGMAN. 'E's a good lad is our Adam, but 'e's down in the
dumps at the moment. 'Im and Christmas, they used to
sing on street corners with the Band of Holy Joy, every
Saturday night, concertina and all. But some of the lads
found out who they were and started putting bits of rope
in collection boxes; it's put them off outdoor testimony.
But this 'ymn's very moving about hanging and mercy and
so forth. Brings tears to your eyes to 'ear Adam and
Christmas singing it.

JENKINSON *returns.*

JENKINSON. Right?

HANGMAN. Right!

JENKINSON [*sings*].

My brother, sit and think.
While yet some time is left to thee
Kneel to thy God who from thee does not shrink
And lay thy sins on Him who died for thee.

HANGMAN. Take a fourteen-stone man as a basis and giving
him a drop of eight foot . . .

JENKINSON.

> Men shrink from thee but not I,
> Come close to me I love my erring sheep.
> My blood can cleanse thy sins of blackest dye,
> I understand if thou canst only weep.

HANGMAN. Every half-stone lighter would require a two-inch longer drop, so for weight thirteen and a half stone—drop eight feet two inches, and for weight thirteen stone—drop eight feet four inches.

JENKINSON.

> Though thou hast grieved me sore,
> My arms of mercy still are open wide,
> I still hold open Heaven's shining door
> Come then, take refuge in my wounded side.

HANGMAN. Now he's only twelve stone so he should have eight foot eight, but he's got a thick neck on him so I'd better give him another couple of inches. Yes, eight foot ten.

JENKINSON.

> Come now, the time is short.
> Longing to pardon and bless I wait.
> Look up to me, my sheep so dearly bought
> And say, forgive me, ere it is too late.

HANGMAN. Divide 412 by the weight of the body in stones, multiply by two gives the length of the drop in inches. [*He looks up and seems sobered.*] 'E's an R.C., I suppose, Mr. Regan? [*Puts book in his pocket.*]

WARDER REGAN. That's right.

HANGMAN. That's all, then. Good night.

JENKINSON. Good night.

WARDER REGAN. Good night. [*The* HANGMAN *and* JEN-KINSON *go off.*] Thanks for the hymn. Great night for stars. If there's life on any of them, I wonder do the same things happen up there? Maybe some warders on a planet are walking across a prison yard this minute and some fellow up there waiting on the rope in the morning, and looking out through the bars, for a last look at our earth and the moon for the last time. Though I never saw them to bother much about things like that. It's nearly always letters to their wives or mothers, and then we don't send them—only throw them into the grave after them. What'd be the sense of broadcasting such distressful rubbish?

PRISONER C. [*sings from his cell window*]. Is e fath mo bhuartha na bhfhaghaim cead chuarta.

WARDER REGAN. Regular choir practice going on round here tonight.

CRIMMIN. He's singing for . . . for . . .

WARDER REGAN. For the quare fellow.

CRIMMIN. Yes. Why did the Englishman ask if he was a Catholic?

WARDER REGAN. So as they'd know to have the hood slit to anoint him on the rope, and so as the fellows below would know to take off his boots and socks for the holy oil on his feet when he goes down.

PRISONER C. [*sings*]. Ni'l gaoth adthuaidh ann, ni'l sneachta cruaidh ann . . .

WARDER REGAN. We'd better be getting in. The other screws will be hopping mad to get out; they've been there since four o'clock today.

PRISONER C. [*sings*]. Mo mhuirnin bhan . . .

His song dies away and the empty stage is gradually lightened for

Scene Two

The prison yard. It is morning.

WARDER 1. How's the time?

WARDER 2. Seven minutes.

WARDER 1. As soon as it goes five to eight they'll start. You'd think they were working with stop watches. I wish I was at home having my breakfast. How's the time?

WARDER 2. Just past six minutes.

MICKSER'S VOICE. Bail o dhis orribh go leir a chairdre.

WARDER 1. I knew it. That's that bloody Mickser. I'll fix him this time.

MICKSER'S VOICE. And we take you to the bottom of D. Wing.

WARDER 1. You bastard, I'll give you D. Wing.

MICKSER'S VOICE. We're ready for the start, and in good time, and who do I see lined up for the off but the High Sheriff of this ancient city of ours, famous in song and story as the place where the pig ate the whitewash brushes and—[*The* WARDERS *remove their caps.*] We're off, in this order: the Governor, the Chief, two screws Regan and Crimmin, the quare fellow between them, two more screws and three runners from across the Channel, getting well in front, now the Canon. He's making a big effort for the last two furlongs. He's got the white pudding bag on his head, just a short distance to go. He's in.

[*A clock begins to chime the hour. Each quarter sounds louder.*] His feet to the chalk line. He'll be pinioned, his feet together. The bag will be pulled down over his face. The screws come off the trap and steady him. Himself goes to the lever and . . .

The hour strikes. The WARDERS *cross themselves and put on their caps. From the* PRISONERS *comes a ferocious howling.*

PRISONERS. One off, one away, one off, one away.

WARDER 1. Shut up there.

WARDER 2. Shut up, shut up.

WARDER 1. I know your windows, I'll get you. Shut up.

The noise dies down and at last ceases altogether.

Now we'll go in and get that Mickser. [*Grimly.*] *I'll* soften his cough. Come on . . .

WARDER REGAN *comes out.*

WARDER REGAN. Give us a hand with this fellow.

WARDER 1. We're going after that Mickser.

WARDER REGAN. Never mind that now, give us a hand. He fainted when the trap was sprung.

WARDER 1. These young screws, not worth a light.

They carry CRIMMIN *across the yard.*

NEIGHBOUR'S VOICE. Dunlavin, that's a Sunday bacon you owe me. Your man was topped, wasn't he?

PRISONER A.'S VOICE. You won't be long after him.

DUNLAVIN'S VOICE. Don't mind him, Neighbour.

NEIGHBOUR'S VOICE. Don't you forget that bacon, Dunlavin.

DUNLAVIN'S VOICE. I forgot to tell you, Neighbour.

NEIGHBOUR'S VOICE. What did you forget to tell me?

ENGLISH VOICE. Where's the bloke what's going out this morning?

NEIGHBOUR'S VOICE. He's up in Nelly's room behind the clock. What about that bacon, Dunlavin?

ENGLISH VOICE. You bloke that's going out this morning, remember to see my chiner and tell him to 'ave me bailed out.

NEIGHBOUR'S VOICE. Get a bucket and bail yourself out. What about me bacon, Dunlavin?

ENGLISH VOICE. Sod you and your bleeding bacon.

DUNLAVIN'S VOICE. Shut up a minute about your bail, till I tell Neighbour about his bet.

NEIGHBOUR'S VOICE. You lost it, that's all I know.

DUNLAVIN'S VOICE. Yes, but the doctor told me that me stomach was out of order; he's put me on a milk diet.

CHIEF [*comes through prison gates and looks up*]. Get down from those windows. Get down at once. [*He beckons inside and* PRISONERS A., B., C. *and* D. *file past him and go down on the steps.* PRISONER B. *is carrying a cold hammer and chisel.*] Hey, you there in front, have you the cold chisel and hammer?

PRISONER B. Yes, sir.

CHIEF. You other three, the shovels are where you left them; get to work there and clear the top and have it ready for filling in.

> They go on to the canvas, take up the shovels from behind and begin work. PRISONER B. stands on the foot of the steps with his cold chisel while the CHIEF studies his paper to give final instructions.

CHIEF. Yes, that's it. You're to carve E.777. Got that?

PRISONER B. Yes, sir. E.777.

CHIEF. That's it. It should be E.779 according to the book, but a "7" is easier for you to do than a "9". Right, the stone in the wall that's nearest to the spot. Go ahead now. [*Raising his voice.*] There's the usual two bottles of stout a man, but only if you work fast.

WARDER 1. I know the worst fellow was making this noise, sir. It was Mickser, sir. I'm going in to case him now. I'll take an hour's overtime to do it, sir.

CHIEF. You're a bit late. He was going out this morning and had his civilian clothing on in the cell. We were only waiting for this to be over to let him out.

WARDER 1. But . . . Sir, he was the whole cause.

CHIEF. Well, what do you want me to do, run down the Circular Road after him? He went out on remission. We could have stopped him. But you were too bloody slow for that.

WARDER 1. I was helping to carry . . .

CHIEF. You were helping to carry . . . Warders! I'd get better in Woolworths.

WARDER 2. To think of that dirty savage getting away like that. Shouting and a man going to his God.

WARDER 1. Never mind that part of it. He gave me lip in the woodyard in '42, and I couldn't do anything because he was only on remand. I've been waiting years to get that fellow.

WARDER 2. Ah, well, you've one consolation. He'll be back.

At the grave PRISONER A. *is the only one visible over the canvas.*

PRISONER B. Would you say that this was the stone in the wall nearest to it?

PRISONER A. It'll do well enough. It's only for the records. They're not likely to be digging him up to canonize him.

PRISONER B. Fair enough. E.777.

REGAN *drops the letters into the grave, and goes.*

PRISONER A. Give us them bloody letters. They're worth money to one of the Sunday papers.

PRISONER B. So I understood you to say yesterday.

PRISONER A. Well, give us them.

PRISONER D. They're not exclusively your property any more than anyone else's.

PRISONER B. There's no need to have a battle over them. Divide them. Anyone that likes can have my share and I suppose the same goes for the kid.

PRISONER D. Yes, we can act like businessmen. There are three. One each and toss for the third. I'm a businessman.

PRISONER A. Fair enough. Amn't I a businessman myself? For what's a crook, only a businessman without a shop.

PRISONER D. What side are you on? The blank side or the side with the address?

VOICE OF PRISONER BELOW [*singing*].

> In the female prison
> There are seventy women
> I wish it was with them that I did dwell,
> Then that old triangle
> Could jingle jangle
> Along the banks of the Royal Canal.

The curtain falls.

Act II, page 53, line 28 to end and page 54 lines 1-4:

PRISONER C. [*comes to him*], Yes, Thomas?

CRIMMIN. [*gives him cigarettes and matches*]. Here, a couple of cigarettes. Myself and the other screw are going into the hospital for a moment. Divide these cigarettes and let you take a smoke. If the Governor or the Chief or the Principal come, let you not have them in your mouths. Do you understand?

PRISONER C. I understand, Thomas, thanks.

Act II, page 57, line 9:

PRISONER C. God look down on us.

lines 16 and 17:

PRISONER C. Oh sir. I have Irish galore. From the cradle up, sir.

line 19:

PRISONER D. Quite. I understand you.

Act II, page 65, line 15:

CRIMMIN. God look down on us.

Act III, page 74, lines 15 and 16:

GOVERNOR. Qualifications in accordance with Memorandum Seven . . .

Act III, page 81, line 14 and 15:

PRISONER C. [*sings from his cell window*]. It is the cause of my sorrow that I have not permission to visit.

lines 26 and 27:

PRISONER C. [*sings*]. There is no north wind there, there is no hard snow there . . .

line 31:

PRISONER C. [*sings*]. My white darling mavourneen.

★   ★   ★